THE VIRTUAL STUDENT

~

THE VIRTUAL STUDENT

A Profile and Guide to Working with Online Learners

Rena M. Palloff, Keith Pratt

JOSSEY-BASS
A Wiley Imprint
www.josseybass.com

Published by Jossey-Bass
A Wiley Imprint
989 Market Street, San Francisco, CA 94103-1741   www.josseybass.com

Jossey-Bass books and products are available through most bookstores. To contact Jossey-Bass directly call our Customer Care Department within the U.S. at 800-956-7739, outside the U.S. at 317-572-3986, or fax 317-572-4002.

Jossey-Bass also publishes its books in a variety of electronic formats. Some content that appears in print may not be available in electronic books.

Library of Congress Cataloging-in-Publication Data

Palloff, Rena M., 1950–
    The virtual student: a profile and guide to working with online learners/Rena M. Palloff, Keith Pratt.—1st ed.
        p. cm.— (The Jossey-Bass higher and adult education series)
    Includes bibliographical references and index.
    ISBN 0-7879-6474-3 (alk. paper)
        1. Distance education—United States—Computer-assisted instruction. 2. College students—United States. I. Pratt, Keith, 1947– II. Title. III. Series.
    LC5803.C65 P35 2003
    371.3'5—dc21   2002154036

Printed in the United States of America
FIRST EDITION
PB Printing   10 9 8 7 6 5

THE JOSSEY-BASS

HIGHER AND ADULT EDUCATION SERIES

Rena wishes to dedicate this book to my Aunt Frances,
who has read every word we've written,
and
Keith wishes to dedicate this book to my wife, Dianne,
with all my love

CONTENTS

RESOURCES: THE TOOLKIT FOR A SUCCESSFUL ONLINE STUDENT

LIST OF FIGURES, TABLES, AND EXHIBITS

Figures

Tables

Exhibits

WHY FOCUS ON THE LEARNER?

Interest and enrollment in online courses continues to grow. We are no longer in the first wave of online course development. The percentage of undergraduates who took Internet-based distance education courses in 1999–2000 increased to 57 percent (National Center for Education Statistics, 2002). Along with the surge in online learning has come a realization by many faculty that they need to focus on techniques to increase participation and collaborative learning. We have moved beyond the "early adopter" stage. Faculty are now looking for concrete methods to make their courses work. They now know that a course cannot simply be created with the expectation that students will know how to access it, navigate it, and participate to the levels they expect. In other words, they realize that attention needs to be paid to orienting students to learning online in every course they take.

When online learning was in its infancy, the focus in the field was to orient faculty to the use of technology and how to develop an online course. With the realization, however, that in an online course students will not simply know how to engage with the instructor, the material, or one another, the emerging focus is on the student. Online learning, in its best form, is learner-centered and learner-focused. But what does it really mean to be learner-focused in the online environment?

In our own work of training faculty to teach effectively online, we have come to realize that although we talk about the learner as the focus of the process, we too have focused on the instructor. The learner has somehow been left out of the equation.

Why is that? Certainly, all of our courses are developed with the learner in mind, aren't they? Our response is: Not really. We recently conducted an online faculty development course. The group was composed of a mix of new and somewhat seasoned faculty who were making the transition to the online environment. Some had taught a few courses; some had taught none. One member of the group announced that he felt that lecturing was still the best way to reach learners. Consequently, what he intended to do was to videotape himself delivering all of his lectures and then use streaming video to present the lectures to his online students. Another member of the group supported that decision, whereas another expressed horror that an instructor would even think of doing this. The instructor had given no thought to bandwidth issues, let alone the boredom factor of watching an instructor deliver a lecture online. Whose needs were being met here? Was this course being developed with the learner in mind? We think not.

Pedagogy, Andragogy, or Heutagogy?

"Higher education has given priority to the integration of technology into the curriculum. As this has occurred, institutions are faced with the many issues that surround making the lessons succeed technologically. . . . It is, therefore, easy for the instructional design of such curricula to be put on the side while we get technology issues 'under control.' Faculty need to focus on learning theory in the design of instructional technology so that they can create lessons that are not only technology-effective but that are meaningful from the learner's standpoint" (Fidishun, n.d.). Although some faculty may disagree, using the principles of adult learning theory may help move us closer to meeting the needs of the virtual student.

As noted by the National Center for Education Statistics (2002), online learners span an age range from late adolescence to late adulthood. Approaching those learners from the standpoint of how adults learn, also known as *andragogy* (Knowles, 1992), can help bridge the gap between faculty- and learner-centered models of course delivery. We have often been asked why we have referred to our work as *electronic pedagogy* rather than andragogy when what we have been promoting is learner-centered, adult-focused learning. We have avoided becoming enmeshed in this debate by responding simply that what we are promoting is the use of best practices in the online classroom. However, because we have focused on the training of instructors where it is the "teacher who decide[s] *what* the learner need[s] to know, and indeed, *how* the knowledge and skills should be taught" (Hase and Kenyon, 2000) we believed that we fell into the pedagogy category.

As we have looked at this debate anew, however, we have come to realize that what we are promoting as we focus more on the learner and a learner-centered educational process is neither pedagogy nor andragogy, but instead *heutagogy*, or self-directed learning (Hase and Kenyon, 2000). In fact, no matter what terminology is used to describe what should be occurring in the online classroom, the reality is that good online learning involves all three theoretical constructs. The instructor provides the container, pedagogically speaking, through which students can explore the territory of the course and, it is hoped, apply their learning to their lives. In this book, we focus on how to make all that happen by looking at the virtual student, who that person is and what that person needs to succeed in an online course, what the virtual student should expect, and what the instructor should expect from the virtual student. We also provide a range of tips and tricks for fostering the success of the student online.

The focus of the book is primarily "cohort-based" learning, that is, students who begin and end a course together during a quarter, semester, or a seminar scheduled at the convenience of the instructor and students. We have found that the community building tips we use and discuss are difficult to implement in non-cohort situations, such as continuing education courses where students start and end at varying times. This does not mean that some attempts at interactive community building in such courses will not be successful, but it is simply more difficult to implement. We have also found the needs of students enrolled in continuing education courses to be different—often these students are looking for the quickest, easiest way to complete requirements for licensure and the like and are not seeking the level of interactivity that an undergraduate or graduate student or even a corporate employee would seek. Consequently, those working with continuing education students may find some of the material contained in this book helpful, but some material simply may not apply in this situation.

Becoming Truly Learner-Focused

A learner-focused, self-directed approach is based on a core belief that we cannot *teach* but can only *facilitate* the acquisition of knowledge. In our previous writing, we noted that several key characteristics enable an instructor to be successful in the online classroom:

- Flexibility
- A willingness to learn from one's students and others
- A willingness to give up control to the learners in both course design and the learning process
- A willingness to collaborate

- A willingness to move away from the traditional faculty role (Palloff and Pratt, 2002)

How actually to do this is the focus of this book. These characteristics form the core of what we consider to be advanced facilitation skills for online instructors as well as the keys to building community and interactivity online and becoming truly learner-focused.

Audience for the Book

The audience for this book is not only faculty engaged in online teaching and learning but also those involved with developing and designing courses, because the principles and techniques we discuss apply to instructional design with the online student in mind. In addition, those involved in the development and marketing of online programs will benefit from reading this book. In our experience, recruitment and retention of the online student is an ongoing issue in many academic institutions. If recruiters pay attention to who the online student is and what that student needs in order to be successful, recruitment should become an easier task and retention should increase. Finally, those involved in doing e-training in the corporate sector will also benefit from reading this book. Corporate trainers who are moving their training programs online are encountering the same concerns about the online student as instructors in academic institutions. The issue is not whether courses are being offered for credit in an academic setting but rather who is attracted to online learning and who should and should not be there. This book should help corporate trainers make better decisions about which training programs to move to the online environment and how to make those programs truly learner-focused.

Online Learning Across Disciplines

Often as we present to faculty on how to deliver effective online learning, we hear from those who claim that the interactive, community-based approach that we promote cannot be used effectively across disciplines. Janet Donald (2002), in her book *Learning to Think: Disciplinary Perspectives*, notes that some basic questions guide the exploration of content in any discipline: "First, what kind of learning environment does the discipline provide? Second, according to the discipline, what knowledge and higher-order thinking processes are important for students to learn? Third, what are the optimal ways of cultivating these thinking processes? En-

compassing all of the disciplines, a final question is, How can post-secondary institutions promote students' intellectual development in all disciplines?" (p. xi). If
we use these questions as a guide, we believe that the principles we promote for
online education can cross disciplines. Certainly, there are disciplinary differences
in delivery of material and the skills that need to be acquired, but we have seen
good use of interactivity and community building in courses such as accounting,
astronomy, chemistry, and mathematics, just as we have in sociology, psychology,
and organizational behavior.

The issue relates in part to how we see ourselves as faculty in the delivery of
knowledge and information. Donald states, "Faculty of necessity must play an important role in formulating an explanation of the context and process of scholarly
inquiry, how it governs their lives, and how students have the opportunity to engage in this process. . . . But our students tell us that without our taking responsibility to build a scholarly community, they will flounder" (p. 292). The need
to be learner-focused transcends disciplines. The need to engage in community
building does as well.

We primarily teach in the social and behavioral sciences and in business and
computer science. We have worked with many faculty from many disciplines who
are successfully teaching online. Although many of the examples in this book come
from our own experience in teaching online, we believe that the basic principles
we promote are applicable to most disciplines in some fashion.

The Corporate Student

Trainers working in the corporate setting should find much of the material contained in this book applicable to their work. More often, we are hearing that business organizations are seeking more interactivity in their online training programs.
Previously, online training in the corporate sector was delivered in what is termed
web-based or computer-based fashion, that is, the participant interacts only with
a course on the computer but not with other participants or possibly even an
instructor. As business organizations increasingly look to becoming "learning organizations," wherein education and learning are becoming a more valued com-
modity as is the management of knowledge, interactivity in online training is
achieving higher status. In fact, we have been called on to deliver training to trainers in corporate settings regarding increased interactivity online and in building
community within the organization.

In our experience, however, we have found that the motivation to engage in
online training differs for the corporate student. Because he or she is not working
toward a letter grade or degree credit, other motivators are necessary, such as credit

toward promotion, pay, or other benefits. However, the issues we discuss in this book, such as time management, learning styles, and the need for a good orientation to online learning certainly apply regardless of the setting in which the course is being delivered.

Organization of Contents

This book is organized in two parts that are followed by two resource sections. The first part of the book profiles the virtual student. Chapter One answers the question "Who is the virtual student?" by providing a look at the demographics of online students, a predictor of success factors for online learning, and an analysis of what we view to be the social psychology of the online student. Chapter Two goes back to our original work on the importance of participation in a learning community and looks specifically at the student's role in that community. We analyze student-instructor and student-student interaction in the learning community and discuss how to maximize that interaction. We also look at how to express and deliver the content of a course without sacrificing interaction, and we review the important subject of collaboration. Chapter Three deals with the somewhat controversial issue of learning styles and how they apply to online learning, and makes suggestions for ways in which instructors can address all learning styles online without a technology-heavy approach. Chapter Four deals with a variety of issues—geography, multiculturalism, religion, literacy, and gender—and how they affect a student's online learning. Finally, what makes a good student services program for those working online? What kind of support does the online student need from the institution? These are the questions we answer in Chapter Five.

Part Two provides a guide to working with the virtual student. It covers a number of specific issues, concerns, and strategies for doing so. Chapter Six builds on the first section by analyzing the elements of a good student orientation to online learning. What should be included and how should it be delivered? Chapter Seven looks at time and commitment issues, specifically focusing on the development of time management skills. Chapter Eight looks at another controversial issue—assessment and evaluation—and includes a discussion about plagiarism and cheating. Chapter Nine deals with the important issues of copyright and intellectual property as well as other legal issues and concerns. This chapter is not intended to provide the final word on these important topics but rather to provide an overview and guide to their application to the online student. Chapters Ten and Eleven close Part Two of the book. Chapter Ten focuses on attrition and retention, issues that are important to administrators and faculty alike. This chapter also looks at an issue that never fails to surface in discussion with faculty: group size and its impact on online teaching and learning. The chapter emphasizes quality, whether in an online course or an online degree program, as the critical issue in the recruitment and retention of the virtual student. Chapter Eleven pulls together the best practices in online teaching—practices which are truly learner-focused.

We close the book with the Toolkit for a Successful Online Student, which brings together all of the tips, tricks, strategies, and suggestions provided throughout the book. Resource A contains faculty tools and Resource B contains student tools. As we have traveled and worked with faculty across the United States, we have been asked for samples of guidelines for courses or a sample frequently asked questions file to orient students to a course. We created this toolkit in response to these requests. It is meant to sum up the book as well as be a stand-alone piece that faculty, trainers, and instructional designers can use when creating and delivering an online course.

As in our previous books, we feel that our words alone are not enough to convey what we are attempting to say. Consequently, we look to the words of our students and their ongoing contribution to our learning process. As in the past, their unedited quotes from online courses are included in the book to illustrate and explain various concepts. This book was written through their words, experiences, and eyes.

When instructors and students are able to reap the benefits of a well-designed online course, the result is excitement about what is possible in the online realm and about learning in general. The virtual student, after participating in such a course, is often able to reflect on the difference in the quality of relationships formed with the instructor, other students, and the process of collaborative knowledge creation that results. The changing relationship between faculty and their students and faculty and their area of content expertise through interaction with their students online also helps to expand the network through which faculty can learn. Faculty, then, are also virtual students, and this book is for us all.

Acknowledgments

We have been amazed and deeply humbled by how well our work has been received and accepted. To everyone who has sent us e-mails and asked us to speak about our work at conferences and workshops, thank you. In addition, we wish to thank the numerous students and faculty with whom we have worked over the last few years—including our "groupies" in the California Virtual Campus—for their contributions to our thinking and practice. Your contributions mean more to us than you can imagine; we could not have developed the models and ideas that we have without all of you.

We would also like to extend special thanks to the following people: our friends at LERN—especially Bill Draves—for your promotion of our work and your support; Debbie King of Sheridan College for your generous contributions to this book; Pam Hanfelt, Leone Snyder, and Liz Bruch from Capella University—thank you for believing in us and taking us into the fold; Terri Cruz from the Fielding Graduate Institute for your assistance in accessing course archives and for just being who you are; the Southwestern Ohio Council on Higher Education (SOCHE) for helping us test out our ideas through the development of the Online Learning Certificate program and the pilot group who braved the waters to test the program, with special thanks to Santhi Harvey and Beloo Mehra for your enthusiasm and contributions; Alpha Sarmian for your assistance once again with the graphics and for your ongoing work on our behalf; Rita-Marie Conrad of Florida State University for your collegiality and support. To David Brightman and Melissa Kirk, our editors at Jossey-Bass—thank you for your belief in us. It means more than you know.

Last, but certainly far from least, we want to thank our families. Rena wishes to acknowledge Gary Krauss—my perennial cheerleader and support, and Paula, Abe, Keith, and Justin Sklar—all of you are not only my family but my closest friends. Keith wishes to acknowledge his wife, Dianne Pratt; his sons, Kevin and Brian; and Dava, Dynelle, Nora Jo, Brittnie, Alyssa, and Kaylee. All of you are our inspiration, and we could not do what we do without you. You have all touched our lives and our work and for that we are forever grateful.

September 2002

Rena M. Palloff
Alameda, California
Keith Pratt
Bella Vista, Arkansas

ABOUT THE AUTHORS

Rena M. Palloff, Ph.D., is a core faculty member at Capella University's School of Education, where she works with master's degree and Ph.D. students, and adjunct faculty at the Fielding Graduate Institute, where she teaches in the school's completely online master's degree program in Organizational Management.

Keith Pratt, Ph.D., is a core faculty member in the School of Education at Capella University and also teaches at the Fielding Graduate Institute. He was formerly a project manager for Datatel, overseeing software installations in community colleges across the United States.

Drs. Palloff and Pratt have both been appointed to the faculty of the Center for Excellence in Education. In addition, they are managing partners of Crossroads Consulting Group, which works with organizations and institutions in developing and delivering effective online distance learning programs. They are the authors of the Frandson Award–winning book *Building Learning Communities in Cyberspace: Effective Strategies for the Online Classroom* (1999) and *Lessons from the Cyberspace Classroom: The Realities of Online Teaching* (2001). Written for faculty, trainers, faculty developers, and administrators of distance learning programs, *Building Learning Communities in Cyberspace* is a comprehensive guide to the development of an online environment that helps promote successful learning outcomes while building and fostering a sense of community among the learners. *Lessons from the Cyberspace Classroom* builds on the framework presented in the earlier book and provides guidelines and suggestions for teaching and learning online for faculty, students, and administrators. The books are based on the authors' many years of teaching experience in the online environment and contain vignettes and case examples from a variety of successful online courses. Drs. Palloff and Pratt have been presenting this work across the United States and internationally since 1994.

THE VIRTUAL STUDENT

~

PART ONE

A PROFILE OF THE VIRTUAL STUDENT

~

CHAPTER ONE

WHO IS THE VIRTUAL STUDENT?

There is an ongoing debate in the academic world about who is attracted to online learning. It has been assumed that it is predominantly adult learners who take online courses because online learning allows them to continue working full time and attend to their family obligations through the delivery of anytime, anywhere education. The "typical" online student is generally described as being over twenty-five years of age, employed, a caregiver, with some higher education already attained, and equally likely to be either male or female (Gilbert, 2001, p. 74). Online students may be nontraditional undergraduate, graduate, or continuing education students.

However, recent statistics published by the National Center for Education Statistics (2002) indicate that interest and enrollment in online courses spans all age groups. As of December 31, 1999, 65 percent of those age eighteen or younger had enrolled in an online course, indicating the increasing popularity of virtual high school courses. Fifty-seven percent of those considered to be traditional undergraduates, ages nineteen to twenty-three, had enrolled. Those ages twenty-four to twenty-nine enrolled at a rate of 56 percent, and those thirty and older enrolled at a rate of 63 percent. The statistics do agree that fairly equal numbers of men and women are enrolling, and with the exception of American Indians and Alaska Natives (of whom only 45 percent enroll), roughly 60 percent of all races enroll.

Many administrators have embraced online distance learning because they believe it represents a means by which to recruit adult students living some distance away from their campuses. The statistics cited, however, are an indicator that, increasingly, as institutions offer online courses they attract traditional undergraduates in residence on campus and not the geographically dispersed students administrators anticipated (Phipps and Merisotis, 1999). In addition, with the success of virtual high school programs across the United States, increasing numbers of high school students are making decisions about where they will go to college based on how "wired" the institution is and how many online course offerings it has in its curriculum. High school students who have experienced online learning want to be able to continue to learn this way in college.

The fact that online courses are being populated by students who are also taking face-to-face courses on campus is creating a set of concerns ranging from fees to assignment of faculty course loads—none of which is being addressed or resolved easily. However, these issues, although important, are not the focus of this book. Our focus is virtual students—who they are and what they need to be successful online. Instead of looking to demographics to paint a portrait of the online student, we believe faculty, instructional designers, and administrators need to look to the social psychology of online students to determine which ones are more likely to succeed and how to address their needs.

Satisfaction with Online Learning

It would seem obvious that when students are satisfied with their online courses and programs, they are more likely to be successful and to stick with them. The National Center for Education Statistics (2002) reports that undergraduates who participated in distance learning courses were more satisfied with those courses over face-to-face options 22.7 percent of the time. Forty-seven percent reported liking both distance learning courses and face-to-face courses about the same, and 30 percent were less satisfied with distance learning options. These statistics show that work needs to be done to improve the quality of offerings in distance learning. Although the same may be said for face-to-face classes, we contend that by focusing on the learner, the quality of online courses will improve; students will be more satisfied with the results and more likely to stay in the course.

Student retention in online courses has become a significant issue for administrators as they come to realize that these courses and programs are not inexpensive to create and run. Hardware and software are expensive, as are training, support and faculty pay for course development and delivery. Faculty, too, are concerned about retention issues. A community college instructor we spoke to stated that he frequently overenrolled his online courses by about one-third to allow for attrition and so that the administration in his institution would not get upset with his enrollment figures. He also noted, however, that this greatly increased his workload as he attempted to track down the students who were having difficulty getting started or who were eventually going to drop his course anyway.

Studies have noted (Carr, 2000) that the very elements that draw students to online classes—convenience in a busy work schedule, ability to continue to attend to family demands—are the elements that interfere with their ability to remain enrolled. A recent e-mail from a student struggling with this dilemma is a case in point:

This email is being sent to formally let you know that I am unable to satisfactorily complete my course work, and to request that I be dropped from the program. This decision was fostered by many factors, work being one, and the others are family, time, and reality. As I mentioned to both of you this was a life long dream for me. The PhD was to be my swan song, my life statement, my mark. How wrong I was. All these things I expected the degree to afford me was already in my possession.

My family, has provided all the filler I needed for the empty spaces in my life. I guess you might [say] I was seeking an "A" in the wrong subject. I needed this humbling experience to bring me back to my reality. I needed to be reminded that what others think of me is insignificant in light of how my family see me. They stood by and watched me try to juggle time to accommodate this program, and one-by-one in their own special way they came to me and voiced their concerns.

I have truly appreciated the time I spent as a PhD student, though brief; I was once in the game and that will have to do. I wish you both the very best in life, thanks again. *Owen*

The issues involved in student retention will be discussed more comprehensively later in the book. But for now, looking at who virtual students are and what they need from their courses will help to provide a context for the specific suggestions we will be making throughout this book for creating truly learner-centered online courses and programs.

A Portrait of the Successful Virtual Student

Online courses and programs are simply not for everyone. The Illinois Online Network has published a list of qualities that taken together create the profile of the successful virtual student.

Clearly, first and foremost, in order to work virtually, the student needs to have *access to a computer and a modem or high-speed connection and the skills to use them.* Many institutions now publish minimum technology requirements in order for students to complete their online courses. The virtual student needs at least to meet the minimum requirements, if not exceed them, in order to participate online. This is particularly true as we begin to push the limits of bandwidth to include elements such as streaming audio and video. However, it is important to remember that not all students have access to high-speed connections and are thus less able to access and download streaming media and large graphic files. Furthermore, some students—particularly working adults—may be attempting to access their courses from work and may encounter difficulties with security measures such as firewalls. They also have to contend with issues of privacy and confidentiality, conflicts with work time, and copyright and intellectual property as they apply to their workplaces. We recently conducted an online course where this was the case. One student kept sending us e-mails telling us that she could not access the course site. We went through our usual troubleshooting measures with her, asking about the browser she was using and if she had a high-speed connection, and made sure she was typing the correct URL for the course as well as entering her user name and password correctly. It was not until she successfully accessed the course from her home computer that we realized the problem was the firewall installed on the server at her workplace. Luckily, her employer was sympathetic to her needs and was willing to open the firewall to allow her access to her course. However, had she not attempted access from home, we might not have been able to diagnose the problem.

Successful virtual students are *open-minded* about sharing personal details about their lives, work, and other educational experiences. This is particularly important when we ask online learners to enter into learning communities in order to explore course material. Virtual students are able to use their experiences in the learning process and also are able to apply their learning in an ongoing way to their life experiences.

The virtual student is *not hindered by the absence of auditory or visual cues* in the communication process. In fact, he or she may be freed up by the lack of visual barriers that can hinder face-to-face communication. In addition, virtual students feel comfortable expressing themselves and contributing to a discussion through largely text-based means. This does not mean that the virtual student must possess exceptional writing skills to begin online study. Some instructors have found that writing skills improve with ongoing participation in online courses (Peterson, 2001).

Similarly, the virtual student is *self-motivated and self-disciplined.* "With the freedom and flexibility of the online environment comes responsibility. The online process takes a real commitment and discipline to keep up with the flow of the process" (Illinois Online Network, 2002). The virtual student also has the responsibility to communicate to the instructor and others if problems arise. Unlike the face-to-face classroom where the instructor is able to quickly identify who may be having trouble with the course, the signs of a student in trouble online are different but equally obvious.

Instructors need to pay closer attention to the following indicators so that they do not miss them in an online class:

- Changes in level of participation
- Difficulty even getting started with the course
- Flaming other students or the instructor, meaning the inappropriate expression of emotions, particularly anger and frustration
- Dominating the discussion in inappropriate ways (Palloff and Pratt, 2001, pp. 112–113)

Virtual students are *willing to commit a significant amount of time to their studies weekly* and do not see the course as the "softer, easier way" to earn credits or a degree. In so doing, they commit to themselves and to the group that they will participate according to the guidelines set out by the instructor or institution. They recognize that if they do not, they are not only minimizing their own chances for success but also limiting the ability of their classmates to get the greatest benefit from the course. Thus, the virtual student is one who *can and does work collaboratively* with fellow learners in order to achieve his or her own learning objectives as well as the objectives set forth in the course.

Virtual students are or can be developed into *critical thinkers*. They recognize that the instructor acts as a facilitator of the online learning process and that in order to have the best online learning experience, they must take charge of that process themselves. This is an "aha" moment that virtual students are bound to have once they embark on the journey of online learning. Engaging in Internet research or following the trail that another student has suggested for supplementing the material in the course helps the student to see that knowledge creation occurs mutually and collaboratively online, leading to increasing critical thinking abilities.

Brookfield (1987) notes: "Being a critical thinker is part of what it means to be a developing person" (p. 1). The instructor can assist in the development of critical thinking skills by using various instructional techniques such as case studies, debates, simulations, and so on. "When helpers and educators work in these ways, they are encouraging critical thinking. Critical thinking is complex and frequently perplexing since it requires the suspension of belief and the jettisoning of assumptions previously accepted without question. As people strive for clarity in self-understanding, and as they try to change aspects of their lives, the opportunity to discuss these activities is enormously helpful" (p. 10). But it is the student who recognizes, through reflection on the learning that emerges from those activities, that his or her knowledge base and ability to reflect critically is increasing. Furthermore, the *ability to reflect* is another critical quality for the successful virtual student.

Online learning is a transformative experience. The ability to read, reflect, and then respond opens the door to transformative learning; in other words, the student's perspective on what is being studied is transformed (Mezirow, 1990). Reflection often takes the form not only of processing the information presented but also exploring the meaning that the material has for the student's life, the changes that may need to be made to accommodate this new learning. It also means questioning where the ideas come from and how they were constructed. Often this is the element that helps to transform the student into a reflective practitioner (Palloff and Pratt, 1999). Furthermore, in the online classroom, the sharing of reflections transforms not only the individual learner but the group and the instructor as well.

Finally, and probably most importantly, the virtual student *believes that high-quality learning can happen anywhere and anytime*—not just in the face-to-face classroom. He or she does not feel the need to see and hear classmates or instructors in order to learn from them and feels comfortable working in a relatively unstructured setting.

Does This Represent the Ideal?

Does the profile just presented represent the ideal virtual student or the average virtual student? If a student does not completely match the profile, does this mean he or she will not be able to succeed online? We do not think so. Although many traditional undergraduate students—those in the eighteen- to twenty-one-year-old age group—can be successful online, they may not possess all of the qualities listed in the previous section. This does not mean, however, that they cannot be successful. We have found that the younger the students, or the lower the educational level (that is, undergraduate versus graduate), the more structure they need in the online environment. This does not mean that adult or graduate students do not need structure too. Creating structure in the online classroom means that the instructor needs to do such things as the following:

- *Create specific posting times*—that is, state in the course guidelines, for example, that the first response to a discussion question is due online by Wednesday of every week.
- *Be specific about the number of responses to other students' posts required weekly*—that is, determine that a student must respond to at least two other students in the group.
- *Be specific about the nature of the post and delineate what constitutes a substantive post.* "A post involves more than visiting the course site to check in and say hello. A post is considered to be a substantive contribution to the discussion wherein a student either comments on other posts or begins a new topic" (Palloff and Pratt, 1999, p. 100). Many students will post with "good job" or "I agree" or "I like

the way you think." Although this type of post is important for the community-building process, students must be told that only substantive posts will count for the grade in the class.

- *Be specific and clear about all course expectations.* Students need to know exactly how they will earn a grade for the class, including how much of the grade is allocated for online participation and for assignments. Nothing should be left to assumption.

- *Stay on top of student participation and follow up if it changes.* If a student begins to drift away from the discussion or is consistently late with assignments, just as in the face-to-face classroom the instructor needs to follow up to see what might be interfering with good participation in the course and strive to assist the student in removing barriers or solving the interfering problems. This is something that does not often occur in the face-to-face classroom. We recently had a graduate student who was a very active participant in an online course. With three weeks left in the term, he suddenly disappeared from the discussion. We e-mailed him and received no response. After we sent a second e-mail, he called us to report that his brother had suffered a stroke and his attention had been diverted to family concerns. We worked with him to create a way to complete the course successfully and still attend to his family obligations. Had we not noticed his absence, however, we would not have learned about the problem.

Certainly, these suggestions can be helpful for all virtual students, but they can make or break the opportunity for success for the undergraduate. Thus, they are critical components of course design for them. We have found that by implementing clear guidelines and setting clear expectations in our courses, students who do not have the characteristics of the ideal online student to begin with will develop them. They are then prepared to move on to their future courses with a leg up and more readiness to tackle what is expected of them online.

Addressing the Needs of the Virtual Student

Knowing who the virtual student is and what his or her needs are online assists the instructor in designing a course that is responsive to those needs and that is truly learner-focused. If we review again the qualities that make for a successful virtual student, the specific instructional design techniques that will support that characteristic become more apparent:

- *The virtual student needs to have access to a computer and modem or high-speed connection and the skills to use them.*

Although we have seen significant increases in available bandwidth for online courses, and although many people now have access to high-speed connections at home, courses should still be designed with learning outcomes and not the available technology in mind. A recent study (Daniel, 2001) noted that even when access to streaming media and the ability to download it was not a problem, students often bypassed those features when included in an online course. Instead they opted to go directly to the discussion board or a chat room in order to interact with the instructor and their student colleagues, feeling that the streaming media added little to the course. Consequently, we still believe that keeping it simple is the best way to convey the material being studied and that maximizing the use of the discussion board and community building will yield the most satisfying outcomes. When streaming media would serve the learning objectives of a course, the instructor may consider burning CD-ROMs containing audio or video clips so that students with slower or more limited access can still make use of them.

- *The virtual student is open-minded about sharing personal details about his or her life, work, and other educational experiences.*

When we invite the virtual student to help form a learning community with their student colleagues and the instructor, we need to make room for and expect a level of personal sharing that is crucial to the process. By creating social areas in the course, we allow for that sharing to take place. In addition, beginning the course with the posting of introductions, bios, or profiles allows students to start getting comfortable with their colleagues as human beings and not just as names on a screen. Furthermore, by creating assignments that allow and encourage students to bring in their own personal experience, we not only assist in the community-building process but also assist with knowledge retention through direct application of concepts. We will return to a discussion of the student role in the community-building process in Chapter Two.

- *The virtual student is not hindered by the absence of visual cues in the communication process.*

Our work has shown us that both the virtual student and the instructor develop what we have termed the *electronic personality*, allowing them to feel comfortable even without visual cues. We believe that in order for the electronic personality to exist, people must have certain abilities, including these:

- The ability to carry on an internal dialogue in order to formulate responses
- The creation of a semblance of privacy both in terms of the space from which the person communicates and the ability to create an internal sense of privacy
- The ability to deal with emotional issues in textual form
- The ability to create a mental picture of the partner in the communication process
- The ability to create a sense of presence online through the personalization of communications (Pratt, 1996, pp. 119–120)

If students do not have these abilities, they are likely to struggle and may decide that online learning is not for them. For some, all of our efforts at community building are not enough. These students need to be able to physically see and hear their classmates and instructor. This is a matter of preference and learning style, an issue we will return to later in the book. Consequently, we believe strongly that students and instructors should not be forced into the online classroom, but rather should be able to choose whether or not to take or teach courses in this manner.

Conversely, we have seen students who have been so freed by the absence of visual cues that they needed to be reminded about limits and boundaries. Some have shared intimate details of their personal lives that are inappropriate for the classroom, such as problems with a spouse or a child. In this case, it is important to communicate with the student individually and help him or her to contain the sharing. It may also be appropriate to refer a student to an adviser or counselor to deal with the issues raised in the classroom.

• *The virtual student is willing to commit a significant amount of time to his or her studies weekly and does not see the course as the "softer, easier way."*

Students who are taking online courses for the first time often have no idea about the demands of online learning. Consequently, it is important to be clear about expectations and offer some guidelines about how much time students can expect to devote to the class each week. An orientation to the online learning process can also be helpful. When students know what to expect in terms of time commitments and are able to develop good time management skills, the likelihood that they will succeed in the course increases. In Chapter Six we offer suggestions for the creation of a good student orientation to online learning, and we suggest creating a frequently asked questions file or a brief class orientation that can be incorporated into an online class, regardless of what the institution itself offers.

• *The virtual student is or can be developed into a critical thinker.*

Offering activities in the course with the goal of developing critical thinking skills is essential in the delivery of a learner-centered course. Using case studies, simulations, shared facilitation, and jigsaw activities, where students add pieces of information and knowledge to create a coherent whole, helps to develop skills while more fully engaging the learners in the learning process. Collaborative activity "(a) lets a group of students formulate a shared goal for their learning process, (b) allows the students to use personal motivating problems-interests-experiences as springboards, (c) takes dialogue as the fundamental way of inquiry" (Christiansen and Dirkinck-Holmfeld, 1995, p. 1). In addition, students engaged in collaborative learning activities should be encouraged to evaluate those activities, their performance, and the performance of their peers collaboratively. This can take the form of a private e-mail to the instructor that contains an evaluation and suggests grades or a more public debriefing of the activity on the course site. Collison, Elbaum,

Haavind, and Tinker (2000) note in their advice to instructors that the development of critical thinking skills in learners becomes apparent when they—on their own and with one another—begin to use the types of interventions the instructor might use. In so doing, learners begin to realize the importance of sharpening a discussion's focus or thinking more deeply about topics. These authors state: "If you've done a good job of laying the support framework for pragmatic dialogue, the participants begin, at least partially, to facilitate their own dialogue" (p. 203). Consequently, if the instructor lays a good foundation for the course, the virtual student will pick up the ball and run with it. However it occurs, collaborative activity is the heart of a learner-centered online course.

- *The successful virtual student has the critical ability to reflect.*

Reflection—whether on the results of a collaborative activity, on the learning process, or on course content—is a hallmark of online learning. Consequently, the virtual student needs to be encouraged to reflect through direct questions. Also, space must be provided in the course to allow for reflection on the various aspects of online learning. We always create a discussion forum in our courses for reflection and encourage students to post their thoughts there as they go. The reflections may include what they have learned about the courseware in use. They may reflect on the application of a piece of learning to their lives or on the significance of something they have read or found on the Internet. We always encourage them to reflect on the course as they go and then use this formative evaluation material to improve what may be happening in the course at the moment or as summative evaluation material to improve the next iteration of the course. Just asking students to respond to discussion questions and the postings of their peers begins the process of reflection. Students learn that one of the beauties of online learning is that they can take the time to reflect on the material being studied as well as the ideas of their peers before composing their own responses. Encouraging students to compose off-line rather than at the moment also assists with the reflective process.

- *Finally, and probably most important, the virtual student holds a belief that high-quality learning can happen anywhere and anytime.*

The virtual student needs to be flexible and open to new experiences and ideas. If students look for traditional educational experiences, where the instructor is the source of knowledge and direction, in a nontraditional setting such as the online classroom, where knowledge and meaning is co-created through participation in a learning community, it will only lead to frustration. Helping students understand that education online does not occur by interacting solely with the instructor is the first step in this process. The online student can be developed into a lifelong learner, seeking out knowledge wherever it may lie and through interaction with peers, other professionals, and their instructors. The following student post illustrates this concept well:

> I think Rena's point is well taken, and yours is accurate as well . . . with much of the scene setting done before the class begins, during the actual experience, the facilitator can almost be invisible as far as the process is concerned, as long as the class stays on track and behaves appropriately. Rather than direct the experience by leading and asking others to follow, as in most f2f [face-to-face] classes, the facilitator constructs a world to be explored and discovered. If the group loses its way, or seems to be banging its head against a wall, the facilitator can lend a hand and gently redirect in a interventional manner unobtrusive to the discovery and learning processes. At least that's been my experience. *Peggy*

Concluding Thoughts

Table 1.1 summarizes the concepts introduced in this chapter. It links the characteristics of online learners, which can be categorized into seven general areas—access, openness, communication skills, commitment, collaboration, reflection, and flexibility—with instructional techniques that support the development of those characteristics.

Instructors need to help students understand their important role in the learning process. In the next chapter, we will explore the concept of the online learning community in greater depth and discuss the student's important role in its formation.

**TABLE 1.1.   LEARNER-FOCUSED INSTRUCTIONAL TECHNIQUES
TO SUPPORT ONLINE LEARNERS.**

Characteristics of Online Learners	Learner-Focused Instructional Techniques
Access and skills	• Use only technology that serves learning objectives. • Keep the technology as simple as possible so that it becomes transparent to the user. • Be sure that learners have the skills to use the technology for the course through surveys, quizzes, or the completion of technology orientations. • Design web pages that contain only one page of text and graphics. • Limit use of audio and video if you use it at all. • Make sure there is judicious use of synchronous discussion, known as chat.
Openness	• Begin course with introductions, posting of bios, or completion of profiles.

TABLE 1.1.   (*CONTINUED*).

Characteristics of Online Learners	Learner-Focused Instructional Techniques
	• Use icebreaker exercises early in the class to get learners to know one another. • Use experience-based exercises and problem-based learning activities. • Include a social area or student lounge in the course.
Communication	• Post guidelines for communication, including netiquette guidelines. • Model good communication. • Explain what constitutes a substantive post to the discussion. • Encourage participation in the creation of course guidelines. • Follow up with nonparticipants or students whose level of participation changes.
Commitment	• Post clear expectations of time demands for students. • Develop and post clear expectations for assignments, assignment completion deadlines, and means by which a grade will be earned. • Be clear about posting requirements; consider creating a specific posting time line. • Support the development of good time management skills.
Collaboration	• Include case studies, small group work, jigsaw activities, simulations, and rotated facilitation to foster critical thinking skills. • Have students post their assignments to the course site with the expectation that they will provide critical feedback to one another on their work. • Ask open-ended questions to stimulate discussion, and encourage students to do the same.
Reflection	• Impose a twenty-four-hour rule for response to postings to allow for reflective responses. • Encourage students to compose responses off-line and then copy and paste to the course site. • Include a reflections area in the course and encourage its use. • Ask open-ended discussion questions that encourage reflection on and integration of material.
Flexibility	• Vary course activities to address all learning styles and to provide additional interest and multiple approaches to the topic. • Negotiate course guidelines with the learners to achieve buy-in to the course. • Include the Internet as a teaching tool and resource, and encourage students to seek out references that they can share.

~

CHAPTER TWO

THE STUDENT SIDE OF ONLINE LEARNING COMMUNITIES

Wenger (1999) notes that issues of education should be addressed first and foremost in terms of identities and modes of belonging, meaning that it is the social aspects of education and the student's need to belong to a group that are most important. He feels that after these important issues are addressed in an educational setting, the instructor can then turn to the transfer of skills and information. The value of education, according to Wenger, is in social participation and the active involvement in community; social identity drives learning. Communities today, whether face-to-face or online, are formed around issues of identity and shared values (Palloff, 1996).

Not all instructors, nor those who research online learning, would agree with this assessment, however. Frequently, as we present to groups of faculty, there is inevitably one person who voices the opinion that community cannot be built online but only face-to-face. Further disagreement occurs over whether an online class can truly be considered a community and whether the formation of community is an essential component of an online course.

Preece (2000) addresses this issue and notes that if online resources are used only to transmit information to students then an online class cannot be considered a learning community. But when development of community is encouraged, the educational experience is more inspired as strong relationships develop among students.

Defining the Online Learning Community

One of the issues that fuels the debate about whether online learning communities truly exist is in how we define them. Shapiro and Hughes (2002, p. 94) note that "there is no value-neutral or purely administrative or technical way of building culture and community" and believe that this is the weakness of the existing literature on online communities. How, then, are we defining community in the context of an online class? Has our definition of online learning communities changed since we wrote *Building Learning Communities in Cyberspace* (Palloff and Pratt, 1999)? Is there a value-neutral way to contextualize community when discussing online learning?

Descriptions of online communities have evolved from Howard Rheingold's (1993, p. 57) definition, which states, "virtual communities are cultural aggregations that emerge when enough people bump into each other often enough in cyberspace," to a place of knowing that certain features must be present to help the people who are seeing one another frequently there coalesce into a community. Jenny Preece (2000) notes that an online community consists of people, purpose, policies, and computer systems. The people interact socially as they strive to satisfy their own needs or perform special roles such as leading or moderating. The purpose is a shared interest or need, information exchange, or provision of service. The policies are assumptions, rituals, protocols, rules, and laws that guide interaction, and the computer system obviously is the vehicle through which all of this happens.

How does Preece's definition apply in the context of an online class? The *people* involved are clearly the students, the instructor, the program administrators, and the support staff. Their social interaction in the context of the online course forms the foundation of the learning community. The *purpose* is the shared involvement in the online course itself. Even when students are taking a course because it is mandatory, their need to be there and be involved is clear. They are earning credit, or in the case of corporate training, fulfilling the obligations set forth by their employer. Sharing information, interests, and resources is part of what online education is all about. It is the basis of a constructivist form of teaching and learning wherein knowledge and meaning is co-created by the learners and the instructor. The *policies* are the guidelines that create the structure of the online course. The guidelines—if discussed and negotiated to a reasonable degree by the learners and the instructor together—provide ground rules for interaction and participation. They not only dictate how often students will be participating together but also how that interaction will occur. For example, when they agree to a "professional communication" guideline, students indicate that they understand that they will respond to one another reflectively, rather than respond in anger or without thinking. The *computer system* in an online course is the course site where everyone—instructor and students alike—meet on a regular basis to conduct the business of the course. It is likely to be a site housed on a university server and accessed from student homes, computer labs on campus, or public access terminals. The technology serves as the vehicle through which the course is conducted.

Our own definition of online community and how it forms in an online course has not varied significantly since we first presented it and is not dissimilar from that of Preece. We would add a couple of features, however, that distinguish the online learning community from an online community such as a listserv or online group where people meet to share a common interest. Engaging in collaborative learning and the reflective practice involved in transformative learning differentiate the online learning community. In addition, we suggest the following outcomes to determine whether community has formed online and become an integral part of the course:

- Active interaction involving both course content and personal communication
- Collaborative learning evidenced by comments directed primarily student to student rather than student to instructor
- Socially constructed meaning evidenced by agreement or questioning, with the intent to achieve agreement on issues of meaning
- Sharing of resources among students
- Expressions of support and encouragement exchanged between students, as well as willingness to critically evaluate the work of others (Palloff and Pratt, 1999, p. 32)

Is this discussion of online learning communities value-neutral? No, it is not, because we strongly believe in a learner-focused approach to these issues and clearly hold a bias toward a constructivist form of instruction. Our approach is not pure constructivism, though, because we believe that the role and presence of the instructor is critical to the process of forming the community and delivering the class. Finally, the active involvement of the online learner in the formation of community is critical to its successful outcome. So, with this in mind, let us turn our attention to three issues: the role of the learner in the formation of the online learning community, maximizing the interaction in that community, and delivering content without sacrificing interaction.

The Role of the Learner in Forming the Online Community

In our previous books we discussed the role of the learner in the online learning process: knowledge generation, collaboration, and process management (Palloff and Pratt, 1999; Palloff and Pratt, 2001). We did not, however, specifically look at the role the learner plays in forming the learning community. It is interesting to note that even learners have some difficulty understanding the importance of entering into a learning community for the purposes of completing a class. For example, take the following bits of dialogue from a graduate class in education that was made up of a small group of five students. Two of the students expressed concern about a lack of participation on the part of their peers:

This is meant only to be a challenge nothing negative. In this discussion you discuss participation and how "the burden is on the instructor to ensure that students feel welcome and secure, and that their comments and experiences are of value." I felt like Rena and Keith established the participation expectations early in this class and asked everyone to agree with them. This could be considered a learning contract. They have mentioned often how important everyone is to this class and how we need input from everyone. This is such a small class we shouldn't need to create special groups to bond, but we've talked often about building community rapport, as it's the whole point of this class. I'm curious when the burden falls on the students to participate in a regular manner? I hope these questions don't offend anyone, I am simply curious where my fellow students are as there have been no posts claiming personal hardships, etc. And this class is turning into an example of how not to build an online learning community. Many agreed to my statement in the beginning that we should challenge each other, here's my challenge. *Christine*

The following is one student's response:

Actually, the comments over the past two weeks have enlightened me a bit. I have about 92 credits and have two required courses remaining before I begin my Comprehensives Quarter. I have been handling this course like the other many I have taken; trying to stay within a week or so of being on target while trying to provide quality responses when I respond (and of course I fell behind). I admit that I have not really thought about this course from a team perspective, but rather from an individual perspective of learning all that I can and responding to discussion when I can. I am a loner by nature so it does not excite me to engage in face-to-face or online discussion and debate. However, in light of the fact that there are only five members in the course, my classmates have helped me to see the importance of staying up with the discussion thread. Of course everyone needs to know that I worked hard and received a MBA and a MS in Info Systems in traditional programs with only speaking when I was presenting a project, so that is just my nature. But again, I will pull more of myself out into the discussion. *Jeff*

This exchange begins to address the issue of the student role in the formation of the online learning community. It is the instructor's responsibility to set the tone and begin with a set of participation expectations to which students can respond with latitude for negotiation. However, once the basis for participation is established, the students must take the reins with gentle nudging from the instructor to do so.

To do so effectively, the virtual student must be open, flexible, honest, willing to take on the responsibility for community formation, and willing to work collaboratively with others. Let us examine each of these attributes individually.

Openness

We mentioned in the previous chapter that an important characteristic for the virtual student to possess in order to be successful in an online course is openness about personal details of his or her life, work, and other educational experiences. The instructor can encourage students to share this information early on through the posting of introductions and bios. As the course progresses, students can encourage one another to continue to share information and experiences by participating in the social area of the course or by responding in a personal way to the posts of others. Some examples of the type of student-to-student interaction that supports community development follow.

Dr.'s:
     I am very glad to hear that you two co-teach and collaborate on the course progression. This should work very well as Fred and myself have co-learned in almost every course we have taken together. We have found it much more fulfilling to learn as a team and pool our efforts. We have definitely learned much from each other as well as our instructors and classmates.
     Also glad to see familiar names in the course room (hi, Alina). This should definitely be an exciting course with the participants and instructors already starting early.
     Good luck to everyone! *Chris*

Hi Chris, and Fred too, I assume. Glad to see local friends from L.A. in another class. Hope all is well. *Alina*

These comments were kicked off by a welcome message from us, the instructors. However, the students took this discussion a step further by personally welcoming one another, thus beginning to form a strong and supportive learning community.

Flexibility and Humor

Going with the flow in an online course, not being rattled when things go wrong, and even facing the minor crises with humor help to keep the sense of community going. Often students will encounter technical difficulties that hamper their involvement, or life experiences may interfere. It is important to be able to jump back in when the barriers are removed and rejoin the learning process and the learning community. In addition, the virtual student needs to accept the different role of the instructor online and recognize that the deepest learning in an online course comes from interacting with everyone involved. Reaching that level of understanding, and being willing to take on responsibility for creating the learning community as a result, is critical to its formation. Jeff, the student we quoted earlier, posted a final reflection in his course after his interchange with the others about his lack of participation:

The most important thing I have learned from this course is that idea that an on-line learning community is more that just an asynchronous discussion answering experience. After many courses in this format, I did not really get this point. I did well, answered my questions at my own pace, and when I saw interesting comments I responded. This course has taught me the on-line experience is so much greater when there is a link or connection between learners and the instructors, and this is how transformative and self-reflective learning happens. I am currently teaching an on-line course and have put a great deal of effort into developing a "community." I would not have put so much emphasis into this if not for this course. Thanks, *Jeff*

Jeff's post shows that reflective learning occurred as the result of his response to Christine's participation challenge earlier. It also shows great flexibility in his willingness not only to rethink his position on the importance of community online but also to incorporate that thinking into his own work outside of the course. When the virtual student is open and flexible, community happens, and transformative learning occurs as well.

The ability to see humor in text and to laugh at ourselves online is another measure of flexibility. Humor is needed to create a warm, inviting course environment. The problem online is that humorous comments may be misinterpreted because visual cues are absent. Consequently, care in the wording of a humorous comment, the use of emoticons (or text symbols that convey emotion, examples of which can be found in the Toolkit), or bracketing the emotion involved, such as [just teasing here], can help recipients understand the intent of the message. Humor should not be used so much that it trivializes the course. However, if judiciously and respectfully used, it can assist in the formation of a learning community. The following lengthy exchange between us, the instructors, and our students is a case in point. It started innocently on our parts—we were curious about why the students would interact with one another but not with us.

Do Rena and I have Virtual Cooties?

Rena seems to think that the reason no one has commented on our Bios and Intros is that we have "cooties," but I know I don't but she may. So it's okay to comment on mine and I'll leave it up to you about hers. *Keith*

Michele to the guy with Cooties:
Hey Keith, I know that Rena doesn't have cooties, it's a guy thing, right??? *Michele*

Cooties ? May I ask.
Sorry guys, I do not follow. I have learned English at university so basically I have a business English. I have had an American sister-in-law (with Italian origin) for over 18 yrs now but still cooking and sewing are simpler in French (to say the least!). I have looked on the Internet for a definition and an understanding of cooties but I have several interpretations. This is a good example of the difference between information and knowledge. I only have information ! Even, my husband could not help, he said you meant cookies but when I showed him some insects, he did not understand. I feel 18 yrs old when I did not dare asking more information because I could look stupid or feel shy. As someone put it, this term is promising. *Francine*

What a wonderful example . . . of how language can be confusing and misleading. Little girls always said that boys had cooties, meaning germs or something that you could catch from them. Actually, my dictionary says that a cootie is a body louse. So you would stay away from the boys (especially the ones you liked, being a little coy) because whatever they had, you didn't want to catch it. *Michele*

Well from what I remember as a kid, many, many years ago when a boy and a girl were together or near each other and didn't want to touch, they would say you have "cooties" and I don't want to touch you. Maybe someone else can come up with a better definition, but to me they were imaginary bugs that would let ya not touch girls. *Keith*

Francine to all about cooties:
OK I got it. I asked my neighbour who was cutting the lawn what meant cooties. She said it was lice! . . . Then I phoned my sister in law and she gave me the full explanation with my 10 yrs old niece saying yeah about boys in the background. This reminds me of the widget word at the bachelor degree! Sometimes language issues can mean a lot! Thank you for your understanding. *Francine*

Laughing out loud in Alameda!!
I'm loving this conversation! I don't remember cooties being a guy thing as a kid. I remember some girls being referred to as having cooties also. Gee, have I been using the term inappropriately my whole life? Ya know how when a face-to-face group files in for a presentation or a class they leave the first row empty? When Keith and I are presenting and that happens, I always ask the audience if they think we have cooties. If this is really just a guy thing, then I guess I'll have to rephrase and ask if they think KEITH has cooties!!!:-} *Rena*

Okay I Give UP!!!!!!! Okay I'm outnumbered here, I admit I have "COOTIES", I kept it in too long and my "feminine" side has come out and I felt the need to share. I've taken some medicine for them and I should be well soon.:) *Keith*

The result of this interchange was the development of a strong learning community. The group was small but very active and looked forward to their daily exchanges with one another and with us. The humor of this situation and the flexibility of the students in dealing with it supported the development of community.

Honesty

Christine's post, which occurred midway through the course, was a good indicator that an atmosphere of safety had been created, allowing her to feel comfortable in being honest with her peers. That degree of honesty only serves to facilitate the development of community. Her post opened the door to other similar posts. Tanya responded as follows:

I am slightly confused how one can register for a course but not do the course work. You are right . . . in a f2f class we are not required to participate a minimum number of times. However, we are required to do assignments. My understanding is that we are asked to answer discussion questions as part of our assignments. How do you justify taking a class if you do nothing but walk into the classroom on occasion? Isn't this in fact what you are doing? In a f2f course room we are not allowed to pick and choose what assignments we will and won't do. If we did, we would fail and ultimately not earn credit for the course. I guess we can approach education in this manner but then what are we doing? Perhaps just buying credits. My sincere fear is that this type of student behavior is what gives online learning lack of credibility. Is there no program accountability? Anyway, I am not asking you to apologize for anything. We set our own standards of what we want to put into and get out of our endeavors. Thanks for your point of view. *Tanya*

The important thing about both Christine and Tanya's messages is that their communication was honest, yet professional. They may both have been feeling a significant degree of frustration with their peers, but they responded in a way that was designed to engage the others in dialogue about their concerns.

The ability to be honest in an online course needs to be modeled first by the instructor; others will then feel comfortable in following suit. The bits of dialogue we present here were stimulated by posts of our own presenting our concerns about poor participation. Some students could see this as nagging and withdraw further. But when students become equally concerned about the development of a learning community and are willing to jump into the fray in a professional way, their honesty is seen as something in service of community development.

Willingness to Take Responsibility for Community Formation

The need for honesty is closely related to the need for willingness to take responsibility for community formation. Students need to get the message that this is seen as important by the instructor and is a critical component of completing the course. By paying close attention to community development early in the course, the instructor models the skills and abilities required for developing community. Students will then pick up on that and continue the work. Simply interacting with one another is not enough. Students will begin to question levels of engagement, as did Tanya, when they feel that commitment to the formation of the learning community is lacking. When the instructor sets the stage appropriately, the virtual student begins to understand that his or her individual learning process depends on the participation and commitment of the other students in the group. A participant in an online faculty development course said it well:

In understanding the notion of online community, I think we must recognize the fact that no matter how attractive the option of being a sponge, it does not build community. Corals build community by each secreting their resources to build the reef & mutually supporting the group.:) *Santhi*

In Santhi's reflection, the virtual student realizes that this is not an individual effort. The commitment to the learning community grows stronger as the importance of collaboration is realized.

Willingness to Work Collaboratively

Collaboration is one of the key features of the learning community. Participation in an online course is not the same as collaboration. Collaboration goes beyond direct engagement in specific activities and is consistent throughout the course (Mayes, 2001). It is a process that helps students achieve deeper levels of knowledge generation through the creation of shared goals, shared exploration, and a shared process of meaning-making (Palloff and Pratt, 2001). When the instructor asks students at the beginning of a course to share their learning goals for the course, an atmosphere where collaboration can flourish is created. Asking students to discuss their concerns about collaboration and to negotiate the way in which they will work together sets the stage for the collaboration that will occur throughout the course. The following is an example of how that collaborative effort might begin.

For probably as many reasons as people we were pretty quiet last week—and yes, need to pick up the engagement to meet our learning goals. . . . I'm here to learn, and teach, and you will get everything I have to offer that is relevant and I feel comfortable sharing. I also have a very full plate—as do we all—To be honest, I logged on several times when I had snippets of time this week and clicked on the "List unseen" and was somewhat relieved when nothing popped up. Not saying that's right—and of course, I thought it would pick up over the weekend—as it has.

Maybe we can structure our discussion to expect less interaction during the week while we work, do reading, and read any pressing postings, but know that the bulk will happen over the weekend. That may not be reasonable—but truth is the bulk of the time I have to give (online and off) is over the weekend. Thanks for checking in on the personal side. *Peggy*

Sounds as though you have a lot on your plate right now. I can't tell, but I am assuming that your comments about frequency are at least partly directed to me since I initiated this line of discussion with my week #2 reflections. If I in any way said something that you interpreted as disparaging to you or to anyone in the group, please forgive me. That was not my intent.

I was looking at the week as both a participant (who barely participated, which is my own personal disappointment) and as a developer/facilitator. Obviously, as learners, we may have different learning objectives and requirements. I learn better through greater frequency of interaction and feedback on my ideas. I also prefer interaction over the course of the week, not exclusively on weekends. *Michele*

Although there is a somewhat frustrated tone to this discussion, Michele and Peggy are in the process of clarifying and negotiating expectations and learning goals. It can be uncomfortable to work through differences of opinion about how a course should progress and to define each student's needs in that regard, but doing so opens the door to collaboration. Collaboration is sustained throughout the course if dialogue, the critique of assignments, and collaborative work are encouraged. But it is the spirit of collaboration, and not the tasks of collaboration, that sustains the learning community. Students must embrace that spirit in order for collaboration to flourish.

Maximizing Interaction

As we have been noting, simple participation is not enough to create and sustain an online learning community. Certainly, minimum participation guidelines assist in getting and keeping students online. However, just checking in on a regular basis but not contributing something substantive to the discussion does little to support the development of the learning community.

Some students enjoy the addition of synchronous discussion, or chat, as a means of building community. When used judiciously, chat can be a good adjunct to a course. We often suggest, for example, that a small group make use of a chat room in the courseware—the software used to deliver the course—in order to discuss a collaborative project or to have a meeting or brainstorming session. Often what occurs in a chat session is that students will wander into social discourse in addition to discussing the topic at hand. This can help foster community as people get to know each other in real time.

Synchronous discussion should not be the only means for students to engage with one another, however. Some may resist engaging in chat sessions for various reasons, including time constraints, and access issues, such as the use of a dial-up connection, and because chat can be an overwhelming experience if it is not moderated well and if too many students are involved. Text can scroll off the screen rapidly as students become immersed in the conversation, making it difficult to follow the flow. Therefore, it is important for the instructor to determine if chat is going to be a mandatory component of the course or an optional tool used to increase interactivity among those who choose to use it.

Promoting active asynchronous discussion is the best way to support interactivity in the online course. Once students establish a rhythm and begin to actively interact with one another online, they will take the responsibility to sustain it, either through social interaction or in response to discussion questions posted by the instructor. Collison, Elbaum, Haavind, and Tinker (2000) believe that the learners will "internalize [the instructor's] internal monologue as commentator, clarifier, and questioner of thoughts" (p. 204). It is important, then, that the questions posted about course material be created with an eye toward developing and maintaining a high degree of interaction.

The following are suggestions that we feel enhance interactivity and participation (Palloff and Pratt, 1999; Palloff and Pratt, 2001):

- Be clear about how much time the course will require of both students and faculty in order to eliminate potential misunderstandings about course demands.
- Teach students about online learning. We will return to a more complete discussion of orientation for online learning later. At this point, however, suffice it to say that students simply do not know how to learn in an online environment, nor do they simply know how to build community. These are two important elements that should be included in a good orientation to online learning.
- As the instructor, be a model of good participation by logging on often and contributing to the discussion and community formation. Students will walk through the door to community formation if the instructor shows them where it is, and perhaps, opens it for them.
- Be willing to step in and set limits if participation wanes or if the conversation is headed in the wrong direction. Instructors need to set limits with those who dominate the discussion, because they can quash the participation of others.
- Remember that there are people attached to the words on the screen. Be willing to contact students who are not participating and invite them in or invite them back in, as the case may be.

Expressing Content Without Sacrificing Interaction

Although students are often able to sustain interaction with one another—sometimes even ignoring the presence of the instructor—the online course does need to be facilitated or the sense of community will wane. There are ways in which instructors can support and maintain the community as well as ways in which they can actually hinder the development of community. Instructors, particularly those who are new to the online environment and the online teaching process, may feel that their presence is necessary to convey course content. However, this belief may lead an instructor to intervene too much in student discussion, thus blocking the process of inquiry and discovery. In order to deliver content without sacrificing interactivity and the formation of the learning community, the instructor must learn to ask expansive questions and strike a balance between too much and not enough interaction with students. If questions are thought provoking, students will respond both to the questions and to one another, thus maintaining the dialogue. Hudson (2002, pp. 193–194) describes this process well:

> Adult collaborative learning has much in common with thesis writing. It is not spoon-fed problem solving and knowledge assimilation but rather a process of finding and sharing information from almost limitless information resources, and above all, learning the skills of *making that process manageable*. Unlike traditional classroom work, this is a process of meta-learning, or learning how to learn. It involves skills of problem formulation and problem manageability, not just problem solving. It means setting up information structures, not just using the structure provided by a textbook; evolving and exchanging skills, not just applying taught skills to one's own work; using heuristic exploratory analysis, not just algorithms supplied by the curriculum; constructing testing models, not just absorbing them from others; seeing performance in terms of group outcomes rather than personal outcomes; and creating action maps, not just following directions.

Concluding Thoughts

Community, then, and the student's roles and responsibilities in creating it are critical to the online learning process. Despite some of the criticism we have heard about formation of a learning community in an online course, we remain committed to its importance in attaining the outcomes we seek. We feel that the development of a learning community online distinguishes this form of learning from a simple correspondence course delivered via electronic means.

Table 2.1 summarizes students' responsibilities in the formation of community and offers tips for the instructor to facilitate and promote their taking on those responsibilities. One of our students remarked that the instructor in an online course is the architect of the learning community. However, it is the learners who are the structural engineers. The following suggestions shown in the table should make it that much easier for students to take on the structural engineering role in the formation of a learning community.

Paying close attention to the individuals who make up the learning community is critical to its success. In the next two chapters, we will discuss specific issues related to the virtual students who make up a learning community: their learning styles and issues of gender, culture, lifespan, lifestyle, and geography. Online learning communities are made up of diverse groups of people. Faculty need to understand the issues of diversity in the group in order to form and work with the community in an online course successfully. As our understanding of online learning communities has grown, we have realized that one size does not fit all. Consequently, paying attention to diversity when designing and delivering a class can only support the successful achievement of learning objectives for all members. We deal first with learning style, an important issue that has often been discussed in relationship to the delivery of both face-to-face and online instruction.

TABLE 2.1. INSTRUCTIONAL TECHNIQUES FOR FACILITATING STUDENT RESPONSIBILITY IN ONLINE LEARNING COMMUNITIES.

Student Responsibilities in Community Formation	Instructional Techniques to Facilitate Community Formation
Openness: Shares details from work and life outside of school.	• Post introductions and bios. • Create a social space in the course. • Encourage judicious use of chat for socializing. • Model openness and humor.
Flexibility: Develops an understanding of the nature of online learning and a willingness to "go with the flow."	• Be willing to give up control and allow learners to take charge of the learning process. • Involve learners in co-creating learning opportunities. • Orient students to the role of the instructor and responsibilities of the learners in online learning. • Provide opportunities for reflection on the role of the instructor, the student, and the course itself.
Honesty: Is willing to give and receive feedback and share thoughts and concerns as they arise.	• Model open, honest communication. • Orient students to appropriate communication skills and giving and receiving substantive feedback. • Orient students to the realities of online learning.

TABLE 2.1.   (*CONTINUED*).

Student Responsibilities in Community Formation	Instructional Techniques to Facilitate Community Formation
	• Provide opportunities for feedback, such as posting papers to the course site with the expectation that feedback will be given and received, and post evaluations of collaborative activities online.
Willingness to take responsibility for community formation: Demonstrates responsibility by taking charge of discussion and other learning activities.	• Rotate or share the facilitation role with students by asking them to take charge of a week or two of the online discussion. • Rotate leadership of small groups. • Use a "process monitor," or a student who comments on group process and progress on a weekly basis. Rotate this role through the group.
Willingness to work collaboratively: Demonstrates the ability to work with peers in discussion as well as in collaborative small group activities.	• Establish minimum posting requirements and monitor those for compliance. • Grade on participation. • Post grading rubrics that establish guidelines for acceptable participation and posting. • Use collaborative small group assignments and evaluate them collaboratively

CHAPTER THREE

LEARNING STYLES

The topic of learning styles triggers much discussion among faculty. Frequently, we hear concern expressed about how to address all learning styles in an on-line course. Some instructional designers contend that, in order to do so, each activity must be offered in multiple formats. When instructors hear this, they panic and ask, "How in the world will I have the time to create multiple approaches to the same activity with my limited preparation time for my online course?"

We do not believe it is necessary to create several presentations of the same material for students with different learning styles. Instead, if an instructor uses multiple approaches to the material being presented in the *entire online course*, along with various types of assignments, the learning styles of all students will be engaged in the learning process.

Instead of viewing learning styles as narrow, restrictive means through which particular students learn, it is helpful to see them as a specific preference among a number of preferences. The preferred style is how one student is likely to approach the material being studied, but he or she also has access to other styles. They may be somewhat weaker because they are not used as often. These styles can, however, be tapped and developed.

Does an instructor really need to address all learning styles in an online course? The answer is yes. But how that happens is the key.

Defining Learning Styles

Litzinger and Osif (1993) define learning styles as the ways in which children and adults think and learn. Learning styles are sometimes described as the personally constructed filters people use to orient their relationships with the world (O'Connor, 1997). These filters are influenced by factors such as age, maturity, and experience, and thus they may change over time. In addition, the study of learning styles has provided us with categories or groupings of these filters. For example, filters may be categorized by the senses—auditory, visual, or kinesthetic. Some people may respond to auditory information more readily than information presented visually, for example. Other studies of learning styles have focused on a combination sensory and cognitive approach to examine how students process information. One result is Gardner's theory of multiple intelligences (Gardner, 1983), which categorizes learning styles as visual-spatial (ability to perceive the visual), verbal-linguistic (ability to use words and language), logical-mathematical (ability to use reason, logic, and numbers), bodily-kinesthetic (ability to control body movements and handle objects skillfully), musical-rhythmic (ability to produce and appreciate music), interpersonal (ability to relate and understand others), intrapersonal (ability to self-reflect and be aware of one's inner state of being), and naturalistic (ability to use awareness of the natural world and the sciences). Armstrong (1994) examined the use of Gardner's theory in the classroom and came to four conclusions: each person possesses all eight intelligences, the intelligences have the capacity to be developed to higher levels, the intelligences work together in complex ways, and there exist numerous ways to be intelligent. Yet other theorists have looked at the study of learning styles through the lens of gender, noting that males and females tend to approach learning and learning situations differently (Belenky, Clinchy, Goldberger, and Tarule, 1986).

In their review of the myriad studies on learning styles, Claxton and Murrell (1988) noted four main categorizations of the ways people learn:

- *Personality models* look at our personality traits as those that shape our orientation to the world. (The Meyers-Briggs Type Indicator is an example of personality trait measure.)
- *Information processing models* attempt to understand how information is received and processed.
- *Social interaction models* consider issues of gender and social context.
- *Instructional and environmental preference models* look at how sound, light, structure, and learning relationships affect perceptions.

Addressing Different Learning Styles

Underlying learning style research is the belief that students learn best when they approach knowledge in ways they trust. However, an instructor can also design activities that challenge students to develop their skills in another learning preference (O'Connor, 1997). Regardless of which approach or theoretical framework an instructor takes in the issue of learning style, the key is to recognize that differences exist and must be accounted for somehow in an online class. A "one size fits all" approach will not work. It is a mistake to assume that every virtual student looks and feels the same. Although the Internet is viewed as the great equalizer, some accommodation must be made for individual differences, including learning style, gender, culture, and the presence of disability.

Schroeder (1993) notes:

> Faculty nationwide are bewildered and frustrated with the students they see in their classrooms today. Unfamiliar with many of the new characteristics, they see contemporary students as hopelessly underprepared, or less bright or motivated than previous generations. Clearly, the way contemporary students view knowledge and derive meaning are vastly different from those of their instructors. . . . As faculty, we have generally espoused the common belief that students learn and develop through exposure—that the content is all-important. We have been accustomed to a traditional learning process where the one who knows (the teacher) presents ideas to one who does not (the student). . . . This approach may work for us but it may not work for the majority of today's students [pp. 1–2].

Is the issue here poor preparation or differences in learning styles? Schroeder believes that our colleges and universities are experiencing an increasing disparity between faculty and students and between teacher and learner. He suggests that understanding how students learn and where they are in the process can help instructors design learning environments that are more responsive to student needs. Using traditional lecture-based teaching styles does not address all learning preferences.

Offering Different Types of Activities

When we add online teaching and learning to the mix, knowing that it is a different type of student who takes online courses, the picture becomes even more muddied for the instructor. Paulsen (1995) suggested that incorporating activities that are one-alone (activities that are structured for minimal interaction with others), one-to-one (activities that are done in pairs or through e-mail), one-to-many (the use of bulletin boards, where material can be accessed), or many-to-many (the use of computer conferencing techniques) can successfully address all learning styles of the virtual student. Some examples of each of these categories follow:

One-Alone Activities. Doing Internet research, including using online databases and journals, participating in listservs related to course material, receiving information via e-mail from online groups producing information related to course material, and applying prior knowledge or learning are a few such activities.

One-to-One Activities. These include doing independent studies, doing internships, taking correspondence courses, and making learning contracts.

One-to-Many Activities. These include online lectures, whiteboard sessions, and online symposia using audio or video produced by the instructor.

Many-to-Many Activities. These are the most common activities. They include discussion groups, listservs, and the discussion board; debates on critical or controversial issues in the course content (debates can be set up by the instructor or encouraged if the issues emerge spontaneously on the discussion board); simulations (students can work through a real or hypothetical situation provided by the instructor in small groups to explore issues and develop skills); role plays (the instructor can assign roles or students can choose them in order to play out a case or situation assigned by the instructor or spontaneously, in response to a situation presented by a student); case studies (cases can be presented by the instructor for student response or students can be asked to generate cases from their work or lives that they then ask their peers to comment on); and collaborative group projects, which can take the form of small group research projects, discussions of cases, simulations, or role plays. Brainstorming sessions, where students are given a situation and asked to respond quickly with their ideas, either synchronously or over a period of a day or so on the asynchronous discussion board, are another example. Finally, in distributed facilitation students are asked to take some responsibility for the course facilitation by choosing a topic or reading of interest, posting a paragraph or two about their understanding of the topic, and then asking a discussion question or two of the group. This relieves the instructor of the entire burden of facilitating the course, creates another source for collaboration, and builds expertise on the part of the students, with individuals or small groups taking responsibility to teach the others on a particular topic.

If the instructor chooses to incorporate many of these activities in course de-sign, then the learning preferences of most of the students in the group will be ad-dressed. Focusing only on reading and discussion to the exclusion of the rest—as many online courses do—may cause some students who are not oriented to learn-ing in that way to get bored. Using a variety of activities, then, is the best insur-ance against losing students because of learning style issues.

Matching and Mismatching Learning Styles

Claxton and Murrell (1988) note that instructors may choose to match or mis-match activities in a course to a student's learning style, depending on the purpose and goals of the course. They believe that matching activities to learning style is particularly appropriate when working with students who are new to the college experience or who are poorly prepared to learn, because the lowest course attri-tion and most effective learning occur when learning style is matched. However, some mismatching is also appropriate so that students can learn to learn in new ways and bring into play ways of thinking and aspects of self not previously de-veloped.

How might an instructor accomplish both matching and mismatching skills in an online course? O'Connor (1997) notes that technology actually increases the range of activities that an instructor can use to address varying learning styles. He looks specifically at activities in three general categories: *adding alternatives, learning cycles,* and *complex activities.*

When adding alternatives, an instructor makes options available to students for the completion of assignments. In the face-to-face classroom, a student may choose to do a hands-on activity instead of writing a paper, perhaps creating a collage or a work of art that demonstrates the concepts being studied. Online, an instructor may allow a student to create a web page or a PowerPoint presentation instead of writing a paper. Including Internet research in a course also taps into multiple learning styles because students are given the latitude to seek out refer-ences and resources applicable to the content. Simulations and games are other ways to achieve learning objectives.

Learning cycles involve designing systematic sets of activities that facilitate all learning styles before completing an assignment. Different types of learning ac-tivities are incorporated into each phase of the learning process and the mater-ial is organized around themes or problems with an emphasis on the development of a skill set before the student can move on to the next phase of learning. Vari-ous units in an online course can be developed with learning cycles in mind. Sim-ulations, for example, give students an opportunity to develop and demonstrate skills, especially when they carry them out in teams. A simulation in the area of counseling psychology asks learners to take the various roles that may be present on a treatment team, such as counselors, nurses, and family therapists. An actual case is presented to the team with a series of increasingly difficult tasks to complete. With the completion of each task, a learning cycle is completed.

Collaborative projects that require each student to contribute to the final product is another way to incorporate learning cycles into an online course. Another strategy might be to have students submit drafts of assignments as the term progresses or demonstrate the completion of a piece of a project. We have used this approach in working with students completing their master's projects. During each week of the term, we ask them to submit increasingly complex pieces of their final projects and then expect them to give one another feedback on their progress.

Complex activities demand that students approach a topic through the use of multiple skills. The instructor provides broad guidelines for completion of the project and then students organize and complete the project based on their styles and needs. Complex activities usually span the entire term and are helpful in organizing the course. Online complex projects can form the basis of collaborative activity. Students can connect through e-mail or chat to prepare their project, and many software programs can assist in its completion. Some students may choose to contribute graphics to the final product, while others contribute text or organize material. The completion of a collaborative, comprehensive group paper or project is a good example of the inclusion of complex activity into a course. One of us was asked to design a course for nursing students on the use of health care databases. The main course project was for the group to build such a database, which required doing a significant amount of research, developing an understanding of the structure and function of databases, and developing database skills over the term. This kind of complex project is likely to tap into the learning styles of all of the students involved.

Engaging Adult Learners Online

Because learning style preferences change with age, experience, and maturity, it makes sense that the activities designed to engage various learning styles in a traditional undergraduate course would be different from those designed to engage adult learners. Schroeder (1993) believes that when working with undergraduates, beginning with concrete learning experiences and then building toward abstract understanding is an appropriate strategy that engages the learning styles of younger, less mature learners. In other words, activities in an online course can be structured to provide experience first and then the theory on which the experience is based.

Is this different for adult learners? One of the things we know about adult learners is that they tend to be goal-oriented and experience-based. Adults often see learning as the acquisition of knowledge that can be used in practice or for career advancement. The more directly an adult can employ the material being studied, the more likely he or she will retain that knowledge. Consequently, beginning with concrete learning experiences is not necessarily a bad approach when working with adults either.

Where adults and traditional undergraduates do differ is in the degree of structure they need to complete a course successfully. Traditional undergraduates tend to appreciate knowing precisely what is expected of them. They prefer sequential learning tasks and find open-ended assignments, independent projects, or self-designed learning situations somewhat challenging (Schroeder, 1993). However, although adults fare better in situations where there is more ambiguity, it should not be assumed that structure is unnecessary. When working online, not providing structure and leaving things to chance can mean the demise of a course. Even when working with adults, we have found that the more explicit we are about course expectations, the more likely they are to succeed. But adults do well with self-directed and collaborative learning experiences and seem to need less direction and structure in order to complete them. Adult students online have an easier time organizing tasks with one another and working toward a successful outcome.

In discussing the issue of learning styles particularly as applied to adults, Boud and Griffin (1987) assert that we all possess six learning capabilities, regardless of our learning style preference: rational, emotional, relational, physical, metaphoric, and spiritual. Boud and Griffin contend that most of our education is focused on and developed around the rational to the exclusion of the other capabilities. They further note that if the rational, emotional, relational, physical, and metaphoric capabilities are encouraged, then the spiritual element will evolve.

Why is this important in online education with adult learners? Online education continues, for the most part, to be text-based, which can focus on the rational. Consequently, we need to pay attention to ways to facilitate the other dimensions of learning or we risk losing our students. Schroeder (1993) notes that traditional undergraduate students today are also seeking a high degree of personalization. Although he is referring to the face-to-face classroom, the same is true online.

Developing a learning community in an online course and using collaborative activity throughout it is a solid means by which to foster all six learning capabilities. Instructors can appeal to and encourage development of all six in the following ways:

- *Rational:* Presentation of content, course readings, and assignments
- *Emotional:* Inclusion of and encouragement to use emoticons and express emotion in posts; description of real-life events that may contain an emotional component
- *Relational:* Use of the discussion board; beginning the course with the posting of intros and bios; inclusion of a social area in the course
- *Physical:* Ability to work anytime, anywhere; and the creation of a warm, inviting course site
- *Metaphoric:* Use of metaphors to link familiar knowledge to the new, sometimes disorienting, knowledge gained online—for example, naming the social space *The Student Lounge,* or holding office hours online
- *Spiritual:* The depth of relationship and intimacy that can be achieved by participating in a learning community; encouragement to share details of one's life and important occurrences from outside the classroom; ritual celebrations of achievements and losses

Whether working online with traditional undergraduate students or with adult students, the more attention we as instructors pay to the formation of a solid learning community, the more likely we are to tap into all learning styles and preferences. We cannot forget that there are real people attached to the words on the screen and that they are not one faceless entity, but a group of individuals with very different needs in the online course.

Collaborating, Complementing, Integrating

Including collaborative activity in an online course—whether it is through small group projects, simulations, case study work, or other methods—is probably the best way to tap into all learning styles present in the group. Students work from their strengths, complementing one another and integrating material as they go. In addition, collaboration helps promote the following:

- *Development of critical thinking skills.* Collaborative activity does not allow students to assume anything. Assumptions must be supported as well as checked out with peers. Working in a small group helps to deepen the thinking process.
- *Co-creation of knowledge and meaning.* Collaborative activity helps students to broaden their thinking on a topic by sharing and working with all viewpoints in the group. Thus, they engage in a constructivist process through which a new sense of knowledge and meaning about the topic being studied is created.
- *Reflection.* Collaborative activity allows students to take their time in discussing and thinking about the project they are working on together. Of course, some

groups will attempt to throw a project together last minute, usually with poor results. If the group truly engages in collaborative practice, however, taking time to reflect and process helps the group to produce a more meaningful product.

• *Transformative learning.* By promoting reflection, collaborative activity allows students to think about and experience learning in a new way. For many, this is transformative. If students, through collaborative activity, are tapping into some of their weaker learning preferences and developing them, a transformation in the way they approach learning is bound to occur.

Concluding Thoughts

It is clear that instructors do not need to create multiple activities for the presentation of one concept in an online course. Instead, using collaborative means to achieve the same purpose empowers students to explore their own potential as they more fully develop multiple pathways to learning. Table 3.1 summarizes the various learning styles or preferences and the instructional techniques that can be used in the online classroom to engage them all.

We now move on to a discussion of other elements that create the diversity found in an online course: gender, culture, life span, lifestyle, and geography. Just as with learning styles, instructors need to pay attention to these issues if they hope to engage every member of the group, form a solid and successful learning community, and achieve the objectives of the course.

TABLE 3.1.   ONLINE INSTRUCTIONAL TECHNIQUES TO ADDRESS VARIOUS LEARNING STYLES.

Learning Style or Preference	Instructional Techniques
Visual-verbal: Prefers to read information.	• Use visual aids, such as PowerPoint or whiteboard. • Provide outlines or lecture materials in written form. • Use written materials, such as textbooks and Internet resources.
Visual-nonverbal or visual-spatial: Prefers working with graphics or diagrams to represent information.	• Use visual aids, such as PowerPoint, video, maps, diagrams, and graphics. • Use Internet resources, particularly those that contain graphics. • Use videoconferencing.
Auditory-verbal or verbal-linguistic: Prefers to hear material being presented.	• Encourage participation in collaborative and group activities. • Use streaming audio files. • Use audioconferencing.

TABLE 3.1. (*CONTINUED*).

Learning Style or Preference	Instructional Techniques
Tactile-kinesthetic or bodily-kinesthetic: Prefers physical, "hands-on" activity.	• Use simulations. • Use virtual labs. • Require outside fieldwork. • Require presentation and discussion of projects.
Logical-mathematical: Prefers reasoning, logic, and numbers.	• Use case studies. • Use problem-based learning. • Work with abstract concepts. • Use virtual labs. • Encourage skill-based learning.
Interpersonal-relational: Prefers working with others.	• Encourage participation in collaborative and group activities. • Use discussion board. • Use case studies. • Use simulations.
Intrapersonal-relational: Prefers reflection and working with others.	• Encourage participation in collaborative and group activities. • Use discussion board. • Use case studies. • Make use of activities requiring self- and group assessment.

~

CHAPTER FOUR

GENDER, CULTURE, LIFESTYLE, AND GEOGRAPHY

Online learning attracts both men and women, people of all ages, people of all cultures, and people from all over the world. Often in our own experience of online teaching, it is not uncommon to be working simultaneously with students living in Asia, Europe, and all across North and South America. However, although it is seen as a great equalizer, the online environment does not meld all students into one type—in other words, all virtual students are not alike. Their unique needs, created by culture, gender, life span, lifestyle, and geography, require attention from the instructor. In this chapter, we explore the issues involved in all of these categories and offer suggestions for addressing them in the online class.

Cultural Issues

The use of the Internet in teaching and learning has increased the array of educational practices available to instructors. They can offer quality instruction to remote students, reach underserved populations, respond to the diverse learning styles of and paces at which students learn, break down barriers of time and space, and give access to students of different languages and cultures (Joo, 1999). Yet, despite all this, there are cultural issues at play that can affect online classes. McLoughlin (1999) notes that technology is not neutral and that when culture and technology interact, either harmony or tension can be the result.

What are some of the cultural issues that may emerge in an online class and how can an instructor plan for and deal with them? Joo (1999) identifies a number of areas where cultural issues may come into play: content, multimedia, writing style, writing structure, and web design. In addition, the roles of the students and instructor in an online course may also raise some cultural issues. Here is a more detailed description of each of these areas:

- *Content:* Some content may be sensitive, in some contexts, particularly with subjects such as political science, history, and religion. An instructor may design a course that is considered politically correct in Western culture but offensive in another culture.
- *Multimedia:* Although graphic material can help bring some courses alive, the instructor needs to be careful when incorporating graphic material, audio, and video to be sure not to use material that reinforces cultural stereotypes.
- *Writing styles:* In many languages, words and grammar are used to convey different levels of politeness. Some students may be uncomfortable with the informal language that students use in the lounge area of an online course or with the ways in which questions are asked and answered. In addition, submitting assignments in English may pose significant problems for non-native English speakers taking a course from an American institution; they may lack written English skills.
- *Writing structures:* The ways in which ideas are presented and arguments are constructed can also be concerns in some cultures. Translated texts may seem obscure or the translations may not be accurate. If the text is in English, non-native English speakers may have difficulty understanding concepts presented. They may need extra time to compose responses to discussion questions.
- *Web design:* Access to and reading of websites can also be problematic for non-native English speakers. For example, Arab-language speakers generally read from right to left; Hebrew is also read from right to left. These students may have the same tendency when reading material on a website.
- *The role of the student and instructor.* In some cultures it is considered inappropriate for students to question the instructor or the knowledge being conveyed in the course. The co-creation of knowledge and meaning in an online course, coupled with the instructor's role as an equal player in the process, may be uncomfortable for a student from this type of culture. Conversely, a student whose culture is more communal, and where group process is valued, may feel uncomfortable in a course where independent learning is the primary mode of instruction.

How, then, can an instructor be culturally sensitive when designing an online course and avoid some of these problems and concerns? Instructors cannot be expected to become knowledgeable about the cultures of every student who is likely to take the class. However, recognizing that instructional design cannot be culturally neutral is a first step in the process of becoming more culturally competent. Henderson (1996) has identified three main approaches to dealing with cultural issues in instructional design. The first is the *inclusive* or *perspectives paradigm*. This paradigm takes into account the social, cultural, and historical perspectives of minority groups but does so without challenging the dominant culture; thus, it pays lip service to cultural sensitivity. The second paradigm is the *inverted curriculum paradigm*, in which the instructor makes a greater attempt to design components or modules of the course from the minority's perspective. This paradigm does a better job of providing learners with an educationally valid experience from a cultural perspective, but because the focus is on only one module or component of the course, it provides an incomplete or potentially inaccurate view. The third paradigm is the *culturally unidimensional paradigm*, in which the instructor makes no attempt to include cultural difference at all and assumes that the worldviews and educational experiences of all learners are the same.

Clearly, Henderson believes that each paradigm comes up short; none is truly culturally sensitive. Thus, he promotes what he calls an *eclectic paradigm*, which entails designing learning experiences that are flexible and allow students to interact with materials that reflect multiple cultural values and perspectives. McLoughlin (1999) applies this notion to the online classroom by stating that if instructors are able to recognize the capability of students to construct their own knowledge and apply prior experience and their own culturally preferred ways of knowing to the task, then it is likely that a more culturally sensitive online classroom will be created.

The instructor's job, then, in responding to the cultural needs of the virtual student is to seek out, to whatever degree possible, materials that represent more than one cultural viewpoint. When this is not possible, the instructor should encourage students to bring such resources to the online group. Creating flexible assignments and task completion structures can also assist with this process. Asking students to share from their cultural perspectives not only helps students but also increases the cultural sensitivity of the group. Recognizing the different ways in which students might respond to instructional techniques online and being sensitive to potential cultural barriers and obstacles is yet another means by which the online classroom can become more culturally sensitive.

Gender Issues

It has long been speculated that women have a different relationship to computers and technology than do men. Early evidence indicated that women felt more anxiety about using computers and technology than men did and instead preferred group work, consequently believing that online learning might not meet their needs (Callan, 1996). More recent studies, however, indicate that women's anxiety about computer technology is abating (Gillett, 1996; American Association of University Women, 2001; Kirton and Greene, 2001).

Despite the narrowing of the gender gap in online learning, some women continue to feel that the world of technology is foreign territory. Only 28 percent of students majoring in computer sciences are women, down from 37 percent in 1984 (Vu, 2000). Gillett (1996) notes that women seem not to take to the process of communicating through computers as readily as men do. And yet increasing numbers of women are enrolling in online courses and programs because of many other factors we have already discussed: they are convenient, allowing women to work full time, attend to family responsibilities, and avoid the child care costs associated with attending classes outside the home. According to a recent report by the American Association of University Women (2001), 60 percent of online learners are over twenty-five years of age and female.

There are two main theories about gender issues in online communications. The first theory maintains that online communication is more equal and that women (and possibly other marginalized groups) are able to participate and complete thoughts, in effect blurring barriers (Shapiro, 1997). The second theory holds that online interaction is merely a reflection of real-world conversation where men dominate. Men introduce more new topics, ignore topics introduced by women, and provide most of the traffic in a mixed-gender environment (Herring, 1993, 1994). Many of our faculty colleagues have noted that their female students participate in online courses differently—tending to avoid discussion of controversial issues and contributing less to the overall discussion in a course. Based on observations by our colleagues, as well as our own experience, we agree that in online classroom groups where both men and women are present, the female students tend to acquiesce to their male counterparts even though they may have significant contributions to make. Furthermore, the women seem less willing to confront male students when their contributions are off-base or inappropriate. In his work on group dynamics, McClure (1998) notes that the dynamics of groups are different based on gender. In groups composed of women only, participation appears to be more active and balanced. What accounts for these differences and how might an instructor deal with them in an online class?

Herring (1994) studied the postings of both men and women to online discussions and determined that men's postings tended to be more self-confident and aggressive, even to the point of flaming (posting a message that is a personal attack). The male style is adversarial, has more of a tendency toward put-downs, is strong and often contentious, and is characterized by lengthy or frequent postings, self-promotion, and sarcasm. Women's contributions, on the other hand, are more supportive and contain elements of self-doubt. Herring notes that these characterizations represent the extreme in gender differences and gendered behavior. Truong (1993) supports Herring's observations by noting that even though computer networking systems obscure physical characteristics, many women find that gender follows them into the online community and sets a tone for their public and private interactions there. In other words, stereotypical behavior continues online.

According to Lisa King (2000), perhaps, "nothing has changed. The same people who hold power in the real world do so online as well. They are the same people who created and control the technologies that make up the Internet. Only when other groups have a say in how and which new technologies are implemented will the world begin to change." (CPSR Newsletter Online, ¶ 3).

The American Association of University Women (2001) report indicates that women seek an online education not only because it is convenient but also because they want the same fulfillment that higher education provides to residential students. Women seek the satisfaction of learning and the sense of accomplishment that comes with participation in an online program. However, the women surveyed for the report did find certain aspects of online learning discouraging, including the cost of tuition and equipment, the often-difficult course load, and the fact that not all distance learning programs are accredited. In addition, despite its convenience, online learning still takes time away from family. The women surveyed felt they were letting their families down by reducing the amount of time they had to spend with them. Success in online learning was significantly increased if women felt support from their families and their workplaces.

The American Association of University Women report makes recommendations for supporting the success of women in online courses and programs, including expanding financial aid programs to assist part-time students currently unable to qualify because they are taking small course loads; involving more women administrators, teachers, and students in the planning process for online courses; educating policy makers about the difficulties faced by working mothers who want to continue their formal education through distance learning; broadly disseminating information on distance learning to reach populations of women—for example, welfare-to-work participants or older women—who are unlikely to visit traditional sites for information; and probably most important, treating distance learning students as responsible and intelligent beings, not passive educational consumers.

Instructors also need to strive to make their online classes "women-friendly" communities. King (2000) notes that women-friendly spaces consist of an equitable mix of genders and actual participation levels in the discussion that are commensurate with their numbers. To achieve communication in an online class that is balanced and equitable, an instructor can do the following:

- Rotate facilitation among students so that all voices are heard.
- Rotate leadership of small, collaborative groups.
- Incorporate collaborative assignments, which support women's needs for group work and support.
- Communicate privately with male students who dominate the discussion to help them become more aware of the impact of their behavior on the group.
- Confront inappropriate use of language or any behavior that is not seen as promoting equity.
- Hold all students responsible for completing assignments.
- "Call on" students who are not participating by reaching out to them to determine what is interfering with their participation or asking them directly for their ideas on a topic.

Geographical Issues

Keith often jokes that although he lives in the hills of northwest Arkansas, he was able to get high-speed Internet quickly and easily, whereas Rena, who lives in the San Francisco Bay Area, had to fight for over two years to get cable Internet and thus was forced to work on a dial-up connection to teach classes and consult. This irony notwithstanding, the inability to get high-speed access or even dependable dial-up access is a very real factor for people living in remote areas. Furthermore, the expense of a high-speed connection may be too great for some students.

Issues of geography can support or interfere with a student's ability to participate in an online class. The ability to access a class anytime or anywhere may not, in fact, happen if a student is relying on undependable telephone service for dial-up access. Take the examples of rural Alaska and western New York State. In remote Alaskan villages there is often only one phone line and one or two computers available for public use. Individual access to a computer and the Internet is almost unheard of. Furthermore, with weather conditions and issues of distance, telephone service may be extremely unreliable. As a result, the University of Alaska is looking into providing satellite service to remote areas so that people living there can take advantage of online courses. Western New York State is home to many low-income rural communities. Our colleagues in the SUNY system have informed us that often students do not even have telephone service, let alone a computer with a modem. They may, however, have a television and a VCR, allowing for the use of other distance delivery options. Using computer labs at satellite campuses is also an option. Because not all students have equal access to computer resources, instructors need to be flexible in accommodating those with unpredictable access to courses.

Geographical and access issues need to be considered when designing an online course. Courses should be designed with dial-up service in mind. In other words, simpler is better. A student with a dial-up connection is likely to have difficulty accessing web pages that are graphics-heavy, downloading and viewing video clips, downloading and listening to audio clips, and participating in chat or whiteboard sessions. Alternatives should be provided to help students avoid the frustration of working with a slow dial-up. The last thing an instructor or student wants to face is a continuous struggle with technology as the course progresses. Keeping the needs of the "geographically challenged" student in mind while designing courses can help to eliminate problems before they begin.

Issues of Religion and Spirituality

Since we wrote *Building Learning Communities in Cyberspace* (Palloff and Pratt, 1999), we have continued to consider issues of spirituality online. We believe that spirit is the essence of our humanity, and because online learning communities are a vehicle through which human beings connect they are essentially spiritual. In that earlier book, we stated, "Our spirituality helps to increase our level of openness and awareness. The increasing openness with which participants communicate in an online class is spiritual. . . . The connection between people, however that may happen, touches the spiritual core. So, regardless of its faults, the electronic community is a spiritual community" (p. 42).

Religion and the expression of religious beliefs do emerge in the online classroom. It is important for instructors to make room for the spiritual and for the students to live by their religious beliefs as a course progresses. It is also the responsibility of the students themselves to communicate with the instructor about particular issues or concerns that may arise around their practice of religion. For example, even if an online course is open and available twenty-four hours a day, seven days a week, a Jewish student may not be willing to participate on Saturdays. Others may be unwilling or unable to participate during their religious holidays because of the dictates of their religions. The same may be true for the instructor. Consequently, it is a good idea for instructors to ask questions about constraints on participation early in the course, allowing students to express those needs openly.

As we have traveled around the country working with faculty, we have heard questions about the appropriateness of quoting scripture or the Bible in online classes. The concern does not apply to courses offered by religiously affiliated institutions, but it does apply to public or private institutions that are not. Many of the religiously based institutions that we have worked with have done a good job of incorporating religious practice into online courses. They have done so by creating rituals, prayer circles, and references to religious material. When appropriate to the institution, such practices can support its mission as well as the religious and spiritual beliefs of the students enrolled.

Our policy in our own online courses is to allow quoting from the Bible as long as it is appropriately done to support a discussion. Allowing prayer, however, in an institution that is not religiously based is not appropriate. We had one student who, in his final paper for a course on social change, complained that the text was written from an evolutionary rather than a creationary stance and that his fellow students did not respond to his quotations from the Bible, which he had offered during the online discussion. In our response, we supported his religious beliefs but made him aware that he was taking classes in an institution where students held various religious beliefs. Their lack of response to his Bible quotes was actually a sign of respect to him. None of his classmates had complained about his postings, thus showing their respect for his beliefs and his ability to express them. We explained that we hoped he would be as tolerant of their beliefs as they had been of his. He appreciated the feedback and stated that he felt supported by us.

It is important to make room for the practice of spirituality and religion on an individual basis, but with all students taking primary responsibility for their needs in this area. This particular student did just that by expressing his concerns, giving us the opportunity both to support him and to increase his awareness of the needs of others.

Issues of Literacy and Disability

Students with disabilities and students with poor reading and writing skills pose additional challenges in the online classroom. Although online learning allows students with disabilities to be fully included in a community, instructors need to pay attention to issues of accessibility, availability, and support in order to ensure their full participation (Standen, Brown, and Cromby, 2001). Furthermore, compliance with the Americans with Disabilities Act (ADA) is an issue online, just as it is in the face-to-face classroom. Just as with issues of culture and gender, technology is not neutral when it comes to access by those with disabilities.

Because the use of a computer is predicated on the ability to read and write with the help of a keyboard and monitor, accommodations must be made for those who cannot accomplish these tasks. Assistive software—such as screen readers or voice-activated software—helps people with some disabilities to access online courses and programs. But not all courseware is designed to work with assistive software, and this creates significant problems for the virtual student who is disabled.

Because of the use of assistive software, there is a need for standards-compliant HTML coding of course websites. Unfortunately, at the time of this writing, the major courseware companies have not yet incorporated standards-compliant coding into their software, although we are assured that this is coming. Instructors who would like more information about ADA compliance for websites should visit the World Wide Web Consortium's Web Accessibility Initiative (http://www.w3c.org/WAI/) and the federal government site on software coding methods for ADA compliance (http://www.section508.gov).

Thus, once again, as a course is designed the instructor must keep in mind that simpler is better. If graphics, audio, or video are to be used, text alternatives should accompany them in order to make them accessible to a screen reader. Minimizing, or making optional, participation in chat and whiteboard sessions eliminates the concern of the disabled student about gaining access to such sessions. Making transcripts available for any sessions that do happen and giving these students an opportunity to respond to the discussion contained therein helps to create a sense of inclusion for those who cannot participate at the time, either because of disability or geography.

Often we are asked by faculty about how to deal with students who are not disabled but who simply do not have the writing and literacy skills required to participate successfully online. In our discussion of student services (see Chapter Five) we mention that it is important for institutions to provide a writing lab, writing courses, or tutorial services to deal with such students. Writing and literacy issues emerge online just as they do in the face-to-face classroom, but they are more prominent in the online classroom, obviously because the primary mode of communication is writing.

In our classes, we do not correct the grammar and spelling of student posts to a discussion board, but we do expect good grammar and format in written assignments for the course. However, if a student's posts are so poorly written that they are unintelligible, we will contact that student, suggest that he or she compose off-line with a word processor, spell-check and grammar-check the work, and then copy and paste it to the course site. We also strongly recommend that the student get writing assistance to help him or her successfully complete the course and all of its assignments.

On a few occasions we have encountered students whose writing was so poor that the institution had to intervene and suggest that they withdraw from the program in order to concentrate on improving their writing. They were encouraged to reapply and reenter the program after successfully completing a course in basic writing skills. Although these were extreme cases, it is important that guidelines for academic preparation be established and adhered to so that we can build and maintain high-quality online programs that are appealing and challenging enough to retain all the students enrolled. At some point, student literacy becomes an issue of quality and academic standards. If instructors do not deal with this issue, it enables the critics to substantiate their claims that online learning is an inferior form of education.

The Digital Divide

The topics covered in this chapter bear witness to the fact that the digital divide—the gap between access to technology by whites and minority groups—still exists. The digital divide in our view, however, exists not only between whites and minorities but also between women and men, and between those with disabilities and the remainder of the population. In fact, the digital divide is not created just by issues of money (or the haves versus the have-nots), but by differences of any kind. In his 1995 study titled "Falling Through the Net," Larry Irving wrote that information "have nots" are disproportionately found in this country's rural areas and inner cities.

An examination by race reveals that Native Americans in rural areas, including American Indians, Aleuts, and Eskimos, proportionately possess the fewest telephones—thus allowing them far less access to the Internet—followed by rural Hispanics and rural Blacks. Black households in inner cities and particularly in rural areas have the lowest percentages of computers in the home, with inner-city Hispanics also ranking low. Among households with computers, Native Americans and Asians/Pacific Islanders ranked lowest among those also owning modems.

In an examination by age, the single most seriously disadvantaged group includes the youngest households (those headed by people under twenty-five years of age), and particularly those in rural areas. Senior citizens (fifty-five years and older), regardless of where they live, surpass all other groups in telephone ownership but rural seniors rate lowest in computer ownership. Among households with computers, the youngest in rural areas also fare worst in ownership of computers with installed modems, followed by rural middle-aged people and senior citizens.

Generally, Irving contends, the lower the educational level, the lower the level of telephone, computer, and computer-modem ownership by households. Irving believes that as we have moved into the twenty-first century, the gap has widened, not narrowed (cited in Young, 2002). Although growth is occurring in computer access and use among low-income people, African Americans, and Hispanics, the gap continues to widen because fewer members of these groups had computer access to begin with.

To close the gap in online courses and programs, administrators and instructors must first be aware of its existence. Accessibility through computer labs and public access terminals can help economically disadvantaged students participate in online courses. Attention to issues of course design can reduce barriers related to culture, disability, or geography. Sensitivity, attention, and intervention can help eliminate potential barriers caused by gender inequity. In these ways, instructors can help narrow the digital divide rather than contribute to its existence. Table 4.1 reviews the various instructional techniques that can be applied in the service of narrowing the digital divide.

Concluding Thoughts

Although the isolation the virtual student may feel in an online course can be eliminated to a great degree through the formation of an online learning community and with instructor attention to issues of learning style and culture, online students also need to feel they are part of a larger entity. Many have described missing a sense of connection to the institution and say they find it difficult to get their unique needs met by the institution. In the next chapter we turn our attention to the institutional needs of the virtual student, ways to help students feel connected to something larger, and the services that students needs to be successful in an online program.

TABLE 4.1. INSTRUCTIONAL TECHNIQUES FOR NARROWING THE DIGITAL DIVIDE.

Online Access Issue to Be Addressed	Instructional Techniques
Culture: Address and include all cultures in course materials.	• Seek out materials that address a multicultural perspective. • Encourage students to bring multicultural materials into the course or address multicultural viewpoints in assignments and projects. • Use collaborative assignments that allow students to work from and teach about their culture. • Encourage students to talk about their cultural perspective in postings. • Develop cultural sensitivity in teaching and among learners through appropriate feedback to one another and respect for cultural practices.
Gender: Create a "gender-friendly" environment.	• Rotate facilitation to give both men and women an equal chance to be heard. • Incorporate collaborative assignments into the course.

TABLE 4.1.   (*CONTINUED*).

Online Access Issue to Be Addressed	Instructional Techniques
	• Respectfully confront any use of language or behavior that does not promote equity. • Reach out to students who are not actively participating in an attempt to remove barriers that may be gender-related.
Geography: Address issues of access.	• Design course materials with an eye to access and use of dial-up connections—keep courses simple. • Make alternatives available, such as text alternatives for audio or video material. • Provide information to students on free or low-cost means of gaining computer access if access is not available at home.
Religion and spirituality: Create an environment that is respectful of all beliefs and practices.	• Allow for the inclusion of all beliefs in online discussion. • Make allowances for religious practices, such as time off for religious holidays. • Encourage students to take responsibility for their needs in this area through regular communication with the instructor.
Literacy and disability: Address needs of disabled students and those with reading and writing issues.	• Encourage students to compose discussion postings off-line to allow for spell checking and grammar checking before posting. • Provide access to online writing labs (OWLs) for writing support and editing. • Design courses with access in mind—use text alternatives for audio, video, and graphics to enable best use of assistive software, and keep course design simple. • Use Bobby Worldwide to check course site for ADA compliance (http://bobby.cast.org/html/en/index.jsp).

CHAPTER FIVE

WHAT THE VIRTUAL STUDENT NEEDS

Online courses do not exist in isolation. They are a part of a degree or training program that is delivered, for the most part, on a campus or in a corporate setting. Online courses may also exist as part of an online degree program, a continuing education or training program, or a virtual university. No matter how these courses fit into the overall structure of the program, however, they are generally part of a larger institution. So, just as virtual students need to feel a sense of community in the course, they also need to feel a connection to the larger institution in which the course is housed. Their connection to the institution and what they need from that institution are the subjects of this chapter.

A Connection to the Institution: The Missing Link

Many administrators wonder why attrition from online courses is approximately 50 percent of those enrolled nationwide (Carr, 2000). Some feel that the heart of the issue is the quality of the courses offered or the differences in teaching and learning online, whereas others believe that the very life circumstances that draw students to online courses—jobs and family obligations—get in the way of their continuation. However, the role of the institution in the retention of the virtual student cannot be ignored. We will return to a lengthier discussion of recruitment and retention issues in Chapter Ten. Our focus at this point is on the types of services the virtual student needs while enrolled in an online course or program.

What virtual students are seeking from their institutions is no mystery. Strong and Harmon (1997) note that students are seeking the following features in an online distance education program: a program based on the ability to meet the educational needs of nontraditional students; a focus on the learner rather than on the instructor; cost-effectiveness; reliable technology that is easy to navigate and transparent to the user; and appropriate levels of information and human interaction. Virtual students also want to be treated like customers. Rick Skinner of Georgia GLOBE (Georgia Global Learning Online for Business and Education) notes that virtual students are "pretty savvy retail customers" (Carnevale, 2001). This means that they demand quality courses and programs as well as responsiveness both from their instructors and from the institution. For example, if they feel that their needs are not being met in a timely fashion, they may become frustrated and withdraw from the course or program.

Technological Issues and Support

We had a recent experience with one of the institutions where we teach. With only three weeks left to the term, the school installed a new portal system through which students could access their classes and other pertinent information. The installation went well for the most part, but some students found they could no longer access the courses they were enrolled in, or when they posted their posts "disappeared." We were contacted by one student who was extremely frustrated with the lack of support she was getting from the institution on this problem. The title of her e-mail message was "HELP, HELP, HELP!"

After 27 minutes of being on hold, I was finally able to get through to [tech support]. Ugh. I guess they are going to refresh the server. I guess I'm getting a little frustrated because they also have not given me access to my 2 spring courses that were supposed to start yesterday. I've called 4 times (after 15+ minutes on hold) and they keep telling me that I should have access in a couple hours. I guess this is a good test for my patience, but I just hate to get behind in 2 classes already because I have such a busy schedule the way it is. *Teri*

We immediately contacted administrators at the university to inform them of this problem, and their follow-up with the student was almost immediate. Although she still had to wait for tech support to solve her problem, at least she felt heard and her frustration abated. Immediate response to requests for support will help the virtual student feel connected to and heard by the institution.

The virtual student expects to be the focus of the online course or program. He or she is seeking to enter a partnership with both the faculty and the institution that results in the achievement of learning goals (Bates, 2000). Hanna, Glowaki-Dudka, and Conceição-Runlee (2000) explain the difference between a teacher-centered and learner-centered philosophy. In the teacher-centered approach, the organization of the course, content, and activities are devised with minimal input from the learners. It is a lecture-oriented format in which learners may not engage in much discussion among themselves or with the instructor. A learner-centered approach, in contrast, involves a process of engaging the learners in selecting and developing content. There is negotiation about the content and strategy for exploring it. There is a significant degree of interaction among the learners and between the learners and the instructor.

Hanna, Glowaki-Dudka, and Conceição-Runlee add two additional teaching philosophies to the mix: learning community–centered and technology-driven. They define a learning community–centered approach as one that promotes social interaction as an essential component of learning. They warn against technology-driven courses because the interaction there is controlled by the technology and not by the instructor or learners. Interaction in this type of course often takes the form of person to machine rather than person to person. It is technology-driven courses that have given online distance learning a black eye, because they are seen as impersonal and lacking in academic rigor. We believe that a combination of learning community–centered and learner-centered approaches is most successful in keeping learners engaged and involved online.

Integrating Student Services into Online Courses and Programs

Rodney Everhart (2000) adds to this discussion when he states that putting content online is only the beginning of what needs to happen in an online program: "The area of communication most lacking today is access to the larger community of the institution and the resources it offers" (p. 48). Many online learners have limited access to libraries, bookstores that carry academic texts, counseling services, even technical support. Consequently, in planning for the delivery of online courses and programs, the institution needs to plan for and address these issues in a comprehensive and integrated way.

Buchanan (2000) states that online students face challenges and obstacles in tracking down the appropriate contact person for administrative questions and in obtaining registration materials, transcripts, and financial aid forms through telephone and e-mail contacts. There is a gap between the administrative software used on many campuses and the software used to present online courses. Often, it cannot be linked to online courses, creating additional obstacles in registration and grading functions. Although the software issue is being addressed to some degree by those who create courseware, it still can create problems for the virtual student.

Furthermore, these students must often seek out their own guidance and career assistance from resources not associated with the campus. All of these barriers may be contributing to the high attrition rates associated with online courses and programs.

Buchanan maintains that there are ways for the institution to remove the obstacles that online students face, such as providing toll-free access to contact people or liaisons designated to work specifically with virtual students, e-mail help lines for reference and service questions, career assistance through electronic means such as online workshops, and links to library resources and bookstore services.

Buchanan's suggestions form the basis of a well-integrated and comprehensive student services program for the virtual student. In addition, providing students with the ability to access course information, register online, and access an online portfolio of grades and other materials also serves them, helping them to feel connected to the institution at which they are enrolled.

The website in Exhibit 5.1, called iGuide, is from Capella University. It illustrates how all of the services we have been discussing can be provided in one place with easy access for students.

Through this website, students can access their courses as well as a variety of services, including application to the university, financial aid information, the retrieval of necessary forms, synchronous and asynchronous counseling services, course descriptions, records and transcripts, and online tutorials. Important announcements can be accessed so that students are kept in the loop of information and can feel connected to the institution. In addition, students who are considering online learning can take a self-assessment to determine if it might be appropriate for them. A website like this helps to reduce feelings of isolation and removes the barriers to accessing information from a distance.

Additional helpful links located in the iGuide are the link to library services, the bookstore, and a community hall or virtual student union where students can connect with one another to talk about social and other topics. In addition, providing an orientation to the courseware being used—as well as to the instructor's teaching and learning expectations—is a powerful way to help keep the virtual student connected to the institution. The fact that students use iGuide as a means of accessing classes means that this is a place where they go daily. Having everything conveniently available to them in one place assures that students will not have to look far to find what they need to be successful online.

EXHIBIT 5.1. EXAMPLE OF A STUDENT SERVICES WEBSITE.

To Charge or Not to Charge? That Is the Question!

As institutions face growing costs for courseware and the technology infrastructure that supports online courses and programs, as well as for on-campus needs, the issue of what to charge for online courses becomes more critical. In the year 2000, colleges and universities in the United States expected to spend $1.2 billion not only on software but also on computer hardware in academic departments to support teaching and learning (Market Data Retrieval, 2002). Should the virtual student be subject to the same activities fees as the on-campus student? Or should there be a different tuition structure including technology fees instead? Institutions continue to wrestle with these questions as they move further into the realm of online learning.

What we do know is that virtual students question and even resent being charged activities fees when they are unlikely ever to use campus-based resources (Carnevale, 2001). They may be more amenable to paying technology fees if they are made to understand what those fees are for. Instead of charging fees, many institutions set higher tuition for online courses. Students may not complain because they are happy with the convenience of taking courses online. However, they also may not know that they are being charged more than on-campus students. Fee policies range all over the map, from charging the virtual student no fees but higher tuition to charging the same tuition and fees regardless of the possibility of use of services. Buchanan (2000) suggests that institutions consider eliminating segregated fees for services that students will not use, such as for bus transportation, campus student groups, and athletic activities. Student fees are an issue that institutions need to address in a planned way as concerns about recruitment and retention grow, or this too could become a stumbling block in the path of the virtual student.

Developing Appropriate Policies

Online courses and programs are often put in place without consideration of the policy issues that affect them. Because courses and programs have not necessarily been well planned, policies seem to develop after the fact as institutions and their virtual students have problems and concerns. In addition to the fee issues, other issues that require policy development include library use and arrangement for remote library use; tuition structures for out-of-state students; financial aid; participation in and use of labs at remote institutions; proctored exams; security and security breaches, issuance of passwords, and archiving of courses; safety issues; harassment and drug or alcohol use; privacy; expectations for student assignment completion and faculty response time to assignments; grading standards and grading rubrics; expectations for program completion; intellectual property and copyright issues; and problem students.

Once policy statements have been devised in these areas, it is important to publish them on the course website and in print so that students can refer to them when needed, along with contact information for people who can help if a problem comes up in any of these areas.

Basic Writing Skills and Tutoring Services

As we noted in Chapter Four, it cannot be assumed that all virtual students will enter online courses with the writing skills necessary to complete them. Although writing skills are likely to improve as they post to the discussion area, provisions need to be made for students who have writing or other academic difficulties. We do not recommend correcting the grammar and spelling in student posts to the discussion board unless the student's writing skills are so poor that they interfere with the communication of ideas. In our experience of online teaching, we have found that commenting on or editing student posts creates a kind of "performance anxiety" that results in reduced participation. Just as most instructors would not think to correct the grammar of a student who was contributing verbally in a face-to-face class, we would not correct the spelling or grammar in a post because it is the equivalent of speaking in class. However, we demand quality work in assignments, including correct spelling, grammar, and format of papers.

When students attend classes on campus, they often have tutoring services or academic support centers available. This is not always true for the online student. Arrangements can be made with online tutoring and editorial services so that students can work virtually with the services they need. In addition, some institutions provide remedial writing courses or tutoring services through the online program itself. Poor writing skills should not be ignored—the virtual student deserves all of the services provided to the on-campus student. Attention to writing skills and academic quality is not just a service that institutions and faculty can provide—it is a critical component in the development of quality online courses and programs.

Quality Is the Key

It is becoming increasingly clear that the virtual student is searching for and needs high-quality online courses and programs. But how can he or she be assured that the course or program about to be undertaken is high quality? The National Education Association, in conjunction with Blackboard, Inc., has provided a research-driven list of benchmarks for quality programs and courses. The three areas that are most pertinent to this discussion of student services and needs are institutional support, course structure, and student support. The institutional support benchmarks involve planning for and maintaining a strong distance education infrastructure. The benchmarks in the area of course structure are as follows:

- *An advisory program to help students determine their motivation, commitment, and access to minimal technology requirements.* As we discuss in the next chapter, this type of information can be provided simply by posting a self-assessment and a frequently asked questions file.
- *Course information that outlines course objectives, concepts, ideas, and learning outcomes.* Faculty are usually responsible for providing course information. However, it should be possible to post an online catalog of courses that includes not only a description of the course but also objectives and learning outcomes, perhaps along with a sample syllabus. Armed with that knowledge in advance, virtual students are more likely to choose courses that fit into their own learning plan and stick with those courses.
- *Web access to sufficient library resources.* Institutions cannot assume that virtual students will have access to local libraries. Therefore, for students to succeed in their courses, it is essential that institutions provide links to databases and other means for students to access and retrieve library materials.
- *An agreement about expectations for student assignment completion and faculty response.* Again, being as proactive as possible in providing information about policies and expectations will make it more likely that the virtual student will succeed. An essential component of a quality course or program is explaining in advance what is expected of students in assignment completion and what they can expect in terms of faculty feedback. This type of policy needs to be institutional and integrated into every course. We will return to a discussion of communication of expectations in the next chapter.

As for student support, the following suggested benchmarks correlate closely with the elements of a good student services program as we have been describing it:

- *Information about programs, including admission requirements, tuition and fees, technical and proctoring requirements, and student support services.* Together, these form the basis of a good student services program.
- *Hands-on training and information to aid students in securing material through electronic databases, government archives, news services, and other sources.* The integration of library resources is critical to the success of the virtual student. Knowing how to access and use those services is the first step in this process.

- *Access to technical assistance.* Access needs to extend beyond the normal business day because most virtual students access their courses late in the evening or early in the morning.
- *Student service personnel to answer questions and address complaints.* Buchanan (2000) believes that institutions should provide a designated contact person or distance education liaison who is available to the virtual student at regular posted hours.

Dealing with the Needs of the Neediest Students

Although the successful virtual student is seen as a fairly independent learner with few needs to be met by the instructor or institution, not all virtual students operate this way. In our experience, some of our highest-achieving students academically may in fact be our neediest students in the online environment. In the face-to-face classroom, these students can see the nod of a head or the smile on an instructor's face when they make contributions to the discussion. Because this is absent online, their anxiety about whether they are performing well may increase.

We recently had experience with two such students in two different classes. Both seemed to react in much the same way—although their contributions to the course discussion were well thought out, demonstrated good critical thinking skills, and received good feedback from their peers, they would often ask at the end of a post, "What do you think, Rena and Keith?" We also received a great deal of e-mail from both of these students—one asking many questions about her project and expressing a great deal of anxiety about the work she was attempting to complete and the other berating us for not responding to her in class in the way she felt she deserved.

The outcome of both situations, fortunately, was good. The first student finally got started on her project and began sending in the work. The second came to a realization—with the help of her classmates—that the feedback issue was related to her anxiety and need for approval and not what we, the instructors, were or were not doing in the class. If the outcomes had been less positive, however, we would have worked closely with these students to connect them to an adviser or counselor through the institution so that their needs, whatever they might have been, would have been met.

We cannot assume that all of our virtual students will be able to function independently. When they are unable to do so, instructors need to provide them with services that will move them in that direction. Providing guidelines on how and when we will provide feedback as instructors can be helpful in this regard. Here are some examples:

- Students can expect that we will respond to each of their introductions as a way of welcoming them to the course.
- We will respond when a question is directly asked of us, especially if a student draws our attention to it by putting our names in the subject line of the post.
- We will post feedback when a student or group of students is off-track or needs to do more work on a topic.
- We will post feedback when a student or group of students exceeds our expectations in a discussion or on an assignment.
- We will post feedback when someone posts something particularly interesting and we would like to expand that discussion to include other students within it.
- We will post feedback to the discussion at least twice weekly, to make process comments, let the group know that they are on track, or summarize key points.

Including this information in a welcome message to the group can prevent problems, help when students become anxious about their performance in an online course, and assure the group that the instructor is present and paying attention to what goes on in the course.

Concluding Thoughts

Essentially, the virtual student needs all the services that are provided to the residential student. However, close attention must be paid to the additional needs and issues that working at a distance creates, such as feelings of isolation and potential problems accessing resources. The following, then, is a summary of what the institution needs to provide in order to meet the needs of the virtual student:

- A high-quality educational experience
- Access to all services and resources available on the residential campus
- A strong technological infrastructure that is available around the clock, along with technical support
- A cost-effective program
- Learner-centered courses and programs

Table 5.1 summarizes these needs along with the means by which institutions can respond to them.

In the first part of this book, we have painted a portrait of virtual students, describing their role in the formation of an online learning community and discussing what they want and need from the institution that is delivering their

TABLE 5.1.   NEEDS OF THE VIRTUAL STUDENT
AND INSTITUTIONAL RESPONSES.

Virtual Student Need	Institutional and Instructor Responses
A focus on the learner: Courses and programs are developed with the learner in mind and the learner is treated like a customer.	• Programs or courses meet identified learner educational needs. • Courses are learner-focused. • The technology used is reliable and easy to navigate. • The program and courses are cost-effective. • Courses and programs contain appropriate amounts of interaction. • Students are kept informed of what they need to know to be successful in the program.
Training and technical support: Students receive training in the technology in use and have access to support services.	• Training occurs regularly, either online or in person. • Online tutorials and FAQs are posted for easy access. • Technical support is available around the clock or in the evening and on weekends, when students are likely to be working on courses and assignments.
Integrated student services: Virtual students need access to the same services provided to on-campus students.	• An integrated student services program is provided, including advising, registration, financial aid, bookstore, library services, tutoring, and career counseling. • There is an online student union where students can socialize. • There is an announcements or news area where information of importance to students can be posted. • Student service personnel are designated to deal with student needs.
Fees and policy development: Policies that are responsive to virtual student needs should be developed and implemented.	• Fees for services not used by virtual students are eliminated. • Comprehensive policies for virtual students are developed, including but not limited to library use, computer lab use, tuition, online safety and security, and privacy. • Expectations for both students and faculty are developed and publicized, including response times, grading, intellectual property and copyright, and acceptable behavior online.

courses. In Part Two we will take a deeper look at the needs of the virtual student and various instructional techniques for addressing them. To begin with, the virtual student has to be oriented both to the courseware that will be used and to the differences between online and on-site learning. In the next chapter, we will look at the elements of good orientations for the virtual student.

~

A GUIDE TO WORKING
WITH THE VIRTUAL STUDENT

ISSUES, CONCERNS, AND STRATEGIES

CHAPTER SIX

DESIGNING A GOOD STUDENT ORIENTATION

In the second part of the book, we shift our focus somewhat from what the virtual student looks like and needs to how to address his or her specific issues and concerns. In this guide to working with the virtual student, the intent is to suggest instructional techniques as well as institutional approaches to the issues in question. In this chapter, we look at the important issue of orienting students to the online course or program.

Students generally enter an online program with the expectation that courses will be more attuned to their needs as learners than face-to-face classes. This may mean that the courses are more convenient for them because of distance or work and family obligations. Or it may mean that they do not like large classroom situations and are hoping for the increased instructor-student interaction that is possible online. Regardless of what draws virtual students to the online classroom, however, they are for the most part unaware of the demands that online learning will place on them. Because they may enter online programs and courses with expectations that do not match the reality, some institutions now offer online courses to teach students about how to learn online, explaining not just how to use the hardware and software but also what the differences in teaching and learning are and how to be an effective student. Other institutions incorporate mandatory face-to-face sessions to provide an orientation to the program and courses. Whatever the delivery system, however, the assumption behind a good student orientation is the same: to maximize the educational potential for both the online classroom and online student. In this chapter, we review the elements of a good orientation for the virtual student. We also make suggestions for incorporating some orientation elements into online classes whether or not the institution offers a separate orientation program.

Before Getting Started

Before even beginning an online orientation, students need to determine if online learning is the preferred method for them. Gilbert (2001) makes the following suggestion to the potential virtual student: "The first step is to discover whether what you want to learn is offered through distributed learning. Next, be clear about why you want to study at a distance. Then, find out for yourself, before you enroll, whether you're going to be any good at this game" (p. 57).

Instructors often ask us how we can predict whether a student will be successful online. Certainly, we have identified characteristics that seem to apply, but there are no hard and fast criteria for success, or any reliable assessment instruments that can be used to measure the possibility of success. Consequently, prediction of success is often left to self-assessment.

In our Toolkit for a Successful Online Student (see p. 139), we include examples of self-assessments that some institutions are using. Most include a look at skills, goals, attitudes, and abilities, and they can help a student who is on the fence to make a decision about whether to proceed with an online class. However, a self-assessment cannot determine if a student will actually be successful. For example, if a student notes that he or she feels more comfortable with a high degree of structure, online learning should not necessarily be ruled out. Some classes are designed with enough structure that the student would feel comfortable with them. Consequently, if students have enough information about what the particular online class or program really involves, in addition to their own self-assessment material, they will be more likely to make an informed decision.

Elements of a Good Orientation

A comprehensive orientation to online learning, whether conducted online or face-to-face, should review the following (Palloff and Pratt, 2001):

- Internet basics, including how to use a browser, access the course site, use the course management software, save and print material found online, do basic searches on the Internet, and use e-mail

- Basic computer skills, such as the use of word processing software
- What is required to become a successful online learner, including time requirements and time management
- The differences between face-to-face and online courses, including the role of the instructor, the role of the student, and expectations about student evaluation
- Interactions between the instructor and students and among students
- How to give feedback to other students
- Appropriate interaction and communication, including the rules of "netiquette"
- How to get help when it is needed

In the following paragraphs we will look at each of these items individually and provide suggestions for accomplishing them.

Internet Basics

It cannot be assumed that just because a student chooses to take an online class, he or she possesses the skills needed for using the Internet. Nor should we exclude a student who does not have those skills. One of us worked with a student who affectionately called herself a "techno-tard" because she was completely unskilled in using computers, had never sent an e-mail, and was fairly unaware of what the Internet might offer her when she took an online class. She enrolled in the class for the express purpose of improving her skills. Her son provided her with assistance, and her ability to use technology grew substantially as a result. Many people also incorrectly assume that students coming out of high school today are skilled in using the Internet. What we have found is that many younger students can play games online and know how to interact in a chat room, but when it comes to applying Internet-based skills to an online course, they are sometimes lost.

Consequently, it is important that information on the basics of using the Internet be made available to students who need that information before beginning an online class. Furthermore, most students benefit from learning about how to do an online search and how to save material found on the Internet that may be useful for the course. Some institutions use such techniques as Internet-based scavenger hunts or visits to fun websites to teach these skills. Students find what they learn to be very useful in extending and expanding their research abilities not only for their online courses but also for courses they may be taking on campus.

Basic Computer Skills

Although teaching basic computer skills may seem a time-consuming task, it is critical for the virtual student to understand the basics of word processing, including creating documents and copying and pasting material, in order to be successful in an online class. As with Internet skills, a student who is not proficient with word processing software should not be excluded from a class, but the appropriate tutorials or support should be made available. We have often talked students through the basics and encouraged them to seek additional instruction locally—through their community adult education programs, online courses designed to teach computer skills, or other low-cost resources. Devoting a small amount of time and presenting material on this topic in an online orientation—at least to determine the skill levels of the students—can save lots of headaches and struggles later when courses are in progress.

What Makes a Successful Online Learner

It is important for the virtual student to understand the issues and concerns likely to come up in online learning. Time management is an important issue for students to think about before beginning a course. Generally speaking, students who are taking courses face-to-face gauge their time based on when classes meet. They may wait to complete their reading until the day before class or the day of class. The same may be true for completing assignments. But the pacing of an online course is different. Because class never officially "meets" and is ongoing throughout the week, students need to find new ways to pace themselves in order to keep up with reading, posting to the discussion, and completing assignments.

Instructing students in effective time management can help reduce information overload because it helps them deal with reading and posting in manageable chunks. For example, it may be wise for students to enter the course site to "read only," then spend some time in reflection and preparing a response to instructor questions or other student posts. Making this suggestion can reduce the students' anxiety levels as they realize that they do not have to respond at the moment every time they log on. We will return to the issues of time, time management, and time commitment in the next chapter.

Differences Between Face-to-Face and Online Courses

One critical success factor for the virtual student is understanding what is required in the online environment. As we have already pointed out, the online classroom is not a place where teachers teach in the traditional sense and learners learn in the same traditional way. Instead, virtual students are required to take far more responsibility for the learning process and are sometimes required to work in a less structured environment.

Teaching online students about their responsibilities and the expectations for them in an online program and in an individual class helps them get a picture of what online learning is like before embarking on a course, thus eliminating the element of surprise. Once again, this can only increase the likelihood that students will stick with a course through completion, having budgeted adequate time for it and being willing to take responsibility for their own learning.

The virtual student needs to see the instructor as a guide who creates the structure and container for the course, allowing the students to co-create knowledge and meaning within that structure. Students need to understand that the instructor helps them begin a journey of discovery and that it is then their responsibility to follow the map to reach whatever destination is contained in the learning objectives for the course.

Many institutions use rubrics for evaluating student performance in an online class. Including an explanation of grading rubrics and how they are used helps students understand how they will be evaluated and eliminates questions and guesswork about this important area. Examples of grading rubrics can be found in Chapter Eight (Table 8.1) and in our faculty toolkit at the back of this book. It is important to remember that the clearer instructors can be with the virtual student going into a course or program, the less likely that confusion and frustration will result and the more likely the student will be successful in achieving learning objectives.

Interactions Between Instructor and Students and Among Students

Along with an understanding of the instructor and student roles in the online course, there needs to be an understanding of the nature of interaction online. In most online courses, students are expected to post in response to discussion questions created by the instructor, and then to reflect on and post feedback to their peers' responses. Sometimes instructors will ask students to do this in a structured way. For example, they might ask students to use what is termed a *two plus two model of posting feedback*—two positive and two critical reflections on material posted by their peers. Regardless of the model used, going into a course the virtual student needs to understand that interaction is expected. Taking an online course is not a "read only" experience. The comments made by students Christine and Tanya, quoted in Chapter Two, came in response to a student colleague who felt it was fine for her to log into the course site only to see what was new and what resources she could glean from the postings of other students. She felt little responsibility to contribute in the spirit of forming a learning community. As a result, the other students felt cheated out of her ideas and her input and that their learning experience was being limited. Students need to understand their responsibility in the creation of a learning community and the importance of their interaction within it.

In addition, if the institution has policies on instructor interaction with students, that too should be shared during the orientation. For example, some institutions have policies on instructor feedback on assignments and allow for a number of days during which students can expect to receive that feedback. Others have policies on responding to e-mail—for example, that students can expect a response of some sort within twenty-four hours.

Although the instructor role online is different, students need not feel abandoned. Understanding the differences in interaction between the online classroom and the face-to-face classroom can help alleviate potential feelings of isolation and also assist students in fairly evaluating their learning experience online.

In her study of the community-building process in online classes, Brown (2001) notes that students new to online learning tend to spend more time becoming familiar with the technology in use, understanding the new approaches to teaching and learning online, and familiarizing themselves with the content of the course than they do engaging in community building. The participants themselves noted that learning in advance what an online community is, how it is achieved, and its importance in online learning increases the likelihood that they will engage in a community building process. Consequently, it is important in orienting students to online work to include information about community building along with the expectation that they engage in community building in their courses. Information on community building may include the rationale for engaging in this activity, what a well-functioning learning community looks like and can offer the individual student, and the importance of collaboration online.

How to Give Feedback to Other Students

How to give and receive feedback is a subject that cannot be reviewed often enough. Brookfield and Preskill (1999) note that students must be prepared to engage in discussion in a course, and that this is a skill that must be taught. Students do not automatically understand what good feedback entails. They also need to understand the importance of giving and receiving feedback in a learning community. We explained earlier what we consider to be substantive feedback by describing a substantive post: "A substantive post responds to the question in a way that clearly supports a position, begins a new topic, or somehow adds to the discussion by critically reflecting on what is being discussed or moving the discussion in a new direction. Simply logging on and saying 'I agree' would not be considered a substantive post" (Palloff and Pratt, 2001, pp. 79–80). An "I agree" or "Good job" post may help to build community but cannot be deemed substantive feedback.

Consequently, a good orientation program will provide information on the nature of feedback, what constitutes a substantive post, what types of questions students might encounter in their online course, and expectations about feedback to their peers. (Sample guidelines for giving and receiving feedback are included in our student toolkit at the back of this book.) The orientation should also clarify how giving and receiving feedback will figure into the evaluation of their performance. If the institution has a standard policy on how participation translates into a grade, for example, it should be shared with students in advance.

Appropriate Interaction and Communication

An important related issue is teaching students about the rules of "netiquette." Brookfield and Preskill (1999) note that "the rules of conduct and codes of behavior are crucial in determining whether or not students take discussion seriously" (p. 53). Although they are talking about face-to-face discussions, Brookfield and Preskill echo our strong belief that all online classes should begin with the posting of guidelines and expectations. In this way, students will engage in a process of negotiation around them and then buy into the mutually negotiated guidelines so that they serve as a contract between the instructor and all participants for behavior in an online course. Although this subject should be reviewed in every course taken, covering this material in an orientation to an online program is also important.

One way to negotiate ground rules, according to Brookfield and Preskill, is to ask participants to share their reflections about discussions they have been a part of previously and ask what made those discussions satisfying, or not, and how they would like to be spoken to by their peers. We have included such discussions in online orientation programs by asking our students to talk about how they like to receive feedback, how it is and has been most meaningful to them, and then to negotiate a set of ground rules together for how they will give and receive feedback in their class.

As for the rules of netiquette, nothing is more likely to interfere with the needed security and safety of an online course than a student who "flames" other participants or posts inappropriate material in the discussion area. Reviewing netiquette guidelines and having students discuss and agree to these rules begins to develop a code of behavior to which students will be expected to adhere. If someone strays from that code, it is easy for an instructor or program administrator to remind the student about the agreement and use it as a jumping off point for counseling if needed. We have included sample netiquette guidelines in the Toolkit for a Successful Online Student.

How to Get Help

A last but very important subject to include in an online orientation is how and where to get help when needed. If help is only available during certain hours of the day, that information should be clearly communicated to students. It is also important to explain who is responsible for the help process and which questions should be directed where. We spoke to a technical support person at one institution who noted that often the questions received at the help desk were about how to conduct library research or find information on an assignment given in a course. Less often were there questions about such issues as passwords or hardware or software. If this is true at a number of institutions, and we suspect that it is, then it would be helpful for all instructors to provide students with a list of addresses or phone numbers where students can get answers about the various aspects of taking an online course. This information may be shared first in the online orientation and then posted to the institution's website in a public place so that students can refer back to it when necessary. Instructors and support staff, however, should also be prepared to act as "triage" personnel when students call or e-mail with questions that should be referred elsewhere.

Incorporating Orientation into the Online Class

If the institution cannot or does not provide student training about how to learn online, then it becomes the responsibility of the faculty delivering the course to make suggestions for how to be successful in it. In fact, even if there is an institutional orientation, incorporating additional information into the course is still a good idea. Instructors can orient students to an online course in the following ways:

- Hold a face-to-face, hands-on orientation, if possible, to show students the course site and discuss online learning.
- Provide an orientation to the course on the course site or as a first discussion item.
- Provide students with a list of frequently asked questions and responses to those questions.
- Place basic information about how to navigate the course site on the welcome screen or course homepage.
- Send an e-mail message or letter to each student enrolled in the course containing orientation information. (Palloff and Pratt, 2001, p. 43)

Exhibit 6.1 shows the homepage for a course in World Wide Web applications developed by our colleague Debbie King at Sheridan Community College in Wyoming. The exhibit illustrates how King offers orientation material in her course. She created her homepage with "Course Information" as the first icon students see, along with a note that says "Read Me First" to give students a pointer about where to begin.

When students click on that icon, they are taken to another page, shown in Exhibit 6.2, which presents the course syllabus and then breaks out class policies

EXHIBIT 6.1. SAMPLE WELCOME PAGE SHOWING COURSE ORIENTATION MATERIALS.

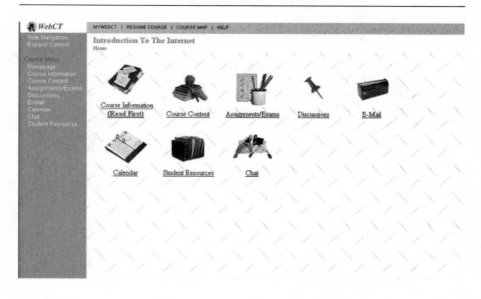

(Exhibit 6.3), computer requirements (Exhibit 6.4), and information on class participation (Exhibit 6.5).

King's site sets out in a clear and well-organized fashion the information students need to begin the course successfully. The orientation material is easy for them to find and covers all the basic issues that we feel are critical for students to understand what is expected of them, where to find what they need, and how to navigate the course.

Concluding Thoughts

Regardless of how it is delivered, an orientation is critical for virtual students if they are to have any likelihood of success in online courses. Instructors and program administrators cannot assume that students will intuitively know how to access a course or navigate it. To create and facilitate high-quality learning experiences for our students, it is the responsibility of all of us to ensure that they are given the best preparation possible. Table 6.1 summarizes the orientation needs of the virtual student along with the techniques we have discussed for addressing them either in a formal orientation program or during the online course.

EXHIBIT 6.2.   SAMPLE COURSE INFORMATION PAGE.

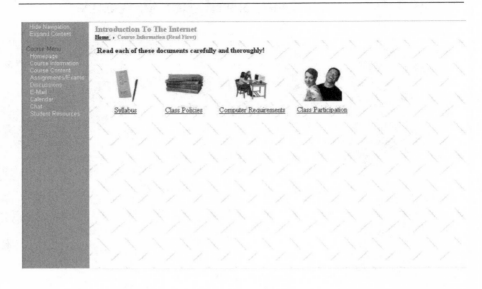

EXHIBIT 6.3.   SAMPLE CLASS POLICIES AND PROCEDURES PAGE.

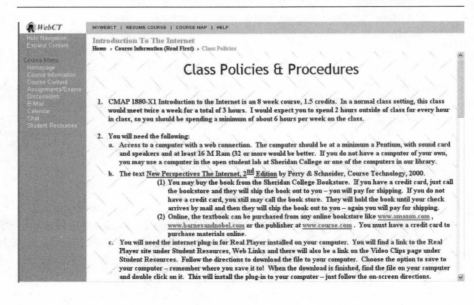

EXHIBIT 6.4.   SAMPLE COMPUTER REQUIREMENTS PAGE.

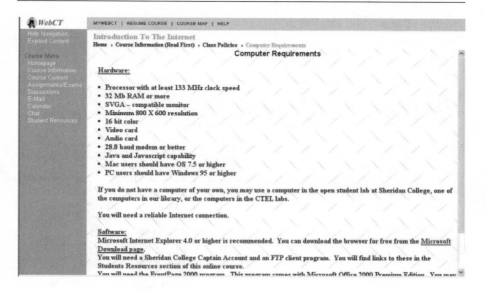

EXHIBIT 6.5.   SAMPLE PARTICIPATION GUIDELINES PAGE.

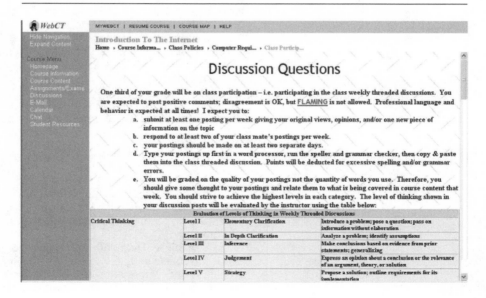

As we mentioned in this chapter, a crucial topic to be covered during orientation is time management. Because this is such an important issue, in the next chapter we discuss at greater length how students can be taught to manage their time in online classes.

TABLE 6.1. ADDRESSING THE ORIENTATION NEEDS OF THE VIRTUAL STUDENT.

Virtual Student Orientation Need	Institutional and Instructor Responses
Program orientation (offered by the institution)	• Provide a self-assessment to determine if online learning is appropriate. • Provide orientation to the courseware in use either online or face-to-face, with online tutorials available throughout the course. • Teach the basics of Internet use. • Teach the basics of online searching and research. • Provide information on the demands of online learning, time management, and differences in instructor and student roles. • Offer information and instruction in appropriate online communication skills, including giving and receiving feedback, netiquette, and use of emoticons. • Provide information on how and where to get help when needed. • Provide information on program and course policies, grading, and expectations of students. • Post course descriptions, syllabi, and faculty bios on the program website. • Provide information about technology requirements for online courses and programs. • Provide information about any course or program policies.
Course orientation (provided by the institution and in the course)	• Post course descriptions, syllabi, and faculty bios on the program website. • Provide specific information on how the course and the course website are organized. • Provide specific information on course expectations, posting requirements, assignments, and grading. • Make available a "Frequently Asked Questions" file about the course and how to complete it. • Provide specific information about what faculty expect of students and what students can expect from faculty. • Provide information on any course or program policies.

CHAPTER SEVEN

TIME AND COMMITMENT

Often, the virtual student does not realize how much time is required to participate in and complete an online course. Instead of being the "softer, easier" way, online courses are actually estimated to require at least twice as much time as regular classes because of the amount of reading and processing involved (Palloff and Pratt, 1999; Gilbert, 2001). Consequently, participation in an online course requires a real commitment to the process not only by the virtual student but by the instructor as well. Although time management should be covered in an orientation to an online course or program, it is worth it for instructors to review the topic during the course as well, because they are likely to be called on to assist students in managing their time as the course progresses.

Basics of Time Management

Typical advice about time management in any setting begins with a focus on goals. Once goals are established, then priorities can be set and time budgeted accordingly. This approach can be useful to the virtual student in planning for the demands of an online course and to avoid feeling overwhelmed. Here is some general advice for the virtual student:

- *Be clear about goals.* Online learning is not the softer, easier way to course completion. It is estimated that a student's involvement in an online course will take twelve to fifteen hours a week (Gilbert, 2001). Therefore, it is critical to plan accordingly.
- *Complete an assessment of how much time is available for online study.* Doing a realistic assessment of how much time it takes to accommodate day-to-day commitments, such as work, commute time, and family time, is important to determine just when in the day there will be time to study and work online. An assessment also helps determine how many classes may be a reasonable number to take in a given term. It is not unusual for us to hear from students that they enrolled in three online classes only to find out that the time demands were so extreme that it was impossible for them to continue.

Setting Goals

A goal-directed virtual student is likely to succeed in online courses. If a student has a clear sense of what he or she wants both from an academic program and every course taken, then the likelihood of staying on track is greater. Adult students may be seeking a certificate or degree to advance their career. Although younger students may not have a career goal in mind, the determination to finish their degree is enough to keep many motivated.

Thus, virtual students should be encouraged to set goals not only for the outcome of their overall programs but also for each course. Even if the course is being taken only because it is a degree requirement, setting realistic goals for that course, along with learning objectives, can help a student determine how much time will be necessary for that course. For example, if the overall goal is to achieve a passing grade in an online statistics course and the objectives include actually gaining a greater understanding of the various subjects studied in the course, the student can assess the course requirements in light of these goals and objectives and then set priorities for independent study, time online, time for assignment completion, and so on. The time allocated for each of these activities can then be marked on a calendar and planned for. Although we suggest that instructors encourage their students to share learning objectives at the beginning of a course to help establish the foundations of a learning community, this activity clearly achieves a second important outcome as well—a first step in time management.

One note of caution, however, when encouraging students to set goals and objectives: they need to be reminded to remain flexible. Online learning takes place in the real world; the student is creating space in his or her own environment in order to make it happen. Life can get in the way of the best-laid plans, goals, and objectives. When other things happen, the virtual student should be encouraged to stay in contact with the course instructor in order not to fall too far behind. The instructor too needs to be flexible and work with students to overcome barriers and obstacles that may well get in the way of course completion. However, the instructor also needs to determine just how real the barriers are. Excuses for not completing assignments have changed in the online world. No longer does the student say, "The dog ate my homework." Instead, instructors are now faced with such excuses as "My computer crashed," or "I accidentally deleted my assignment," or something like this one, which we recently received: "A technician reformatted my hard drive by mistake." Allowing the virtual student a little leeway in working with technical problems is important, but if the excuses crop up often, it is also important to be on the alert and ask questions to determine how real the technical problems may be.

Setting Priorities

Once the student has set goals, then priorities can be set. Students should be encouraged to think about activities in terms of their importance and urgency so that they can determine where the activities involved in their online course might fall. Figure 7.1 can assist students in prioritizing their activities.

Let's briefly consider all the quadrants in the diagram and discuss activities that might fall into them.

Not Important or Urgent

Although many students would say that this category can be ignored altogether, in fact they need to recognize just how much time they spend on activities here. Included are such things as talking on the phone, watching television, or playing

FIGURE 7.1.   PRIORITIZING TIME COMMITMENTS.

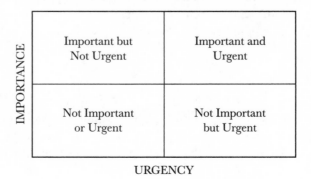

"Spider Solitaire" on the computer. Basically, these are the time-wasting activities that many of us engage in from time to time, and that are used as a break from more rigorous activity or to relax. Students need to keep track of these activities and allow some time for them because even the most motivated student cannot be "on" all the time. These kinds of downtime activities help us to recharge so that we can be productive in other areas. The issue is not to spend too much time on the activities in this quadrant.

Not Important but Urgent

Many of us feel stressed, pressured, and hurried throughout our days and wonder at the end of each day what exactly we have accomplished. Engaging in activities that are not important but seem urgent can make virtual students feel they are simply spinning their wheels and accomplishing little. We have received many frantic e-mails from students who are upset because they cannot do it all. Often, when we engage them in conversation, we find that they are devoting their time to unimportant activities rather than prioritizing what they need to accomplish. Answering the question "What will be the consequences if I don't do this today?" can help to put things in perspective, especially if it turns out that the consequences would be minimal. It is frequently our own perspective on the activity that creates the sense of urgency and not the activity itself.

Important but Not Urgent

This category is a difficult one to work with because these activities tend to get put off until they become urgent. For example, getting a start on an assignment or a paper is important, but if the deadline is weeks away, it is not urgent. Encouraging students to pay attention to aspects of the course that have long deadlines may not be easy, but for managing time in the long run it will be beneficial. For example, it can be helpful to suggest that students put all of the assignments for the course on a calendar and create a time line for assignment completion that takes them through the term and helps keep them on track. In this way, important activities do not get lost among more urgent matters.

Important and Urgent

Many students (and many of us in general) are motivated by urgency. Waiting until the last minute to post an assignment, complete a paper, or respond to the online discussion increases the importance and urgency of that work. However, when students operate out of this quadrant almost entirely, the notion of building a learning community can be lost. For example, if a student waits until weekends to post assignments and most of the other students have already posted, the others may feel cheated by missing out on the contributions of the late arrivals. Many virtual students, like their counterparts in the face-to-face classroom, opt to take weekends off, which can also create significant breaks in community development. Here is how one student reacted to this situation in an online class:

This week, I felt as though we had monologues, as opposed to dialogues. I posted my ideas and no one commented on them by Saturday morning. I started thinking (a) is there something wrong with me or the ideas that I expressed (b) is there something wrong with them? Are they busy? Do they not like me? Have I inadvertently done or said something that would prevent them from wanting to engage in conversation with me? I may be exaggerating a bit because as a more experienced online learner, I know that stuff happens and things sometimes take priority over the class, no matter how good our intentions, but if I were new to online learning, I might be thinking—oh no, this is not going to work. It makes me wonder. Could we agree, if we will not be able to post anything, that we will at least check in and let the group know. Maybe we should add this to our guidelines? As our relationships begin to grow and we begin to care about each other's well-being, it helps to know where someone is and if they are okay. *Michele*

Managing time well and setting priorities for dealing with the demands of an online course are critical to the formation of a learning community. If students do not make a commitment to put their studies ahead of other unimportant and nonurgent activities, the other members of the group will suffer by their absence.

Budgeting Time for Studying and Interacting Online

Gilbert (2001) notes that there are documented efficient means for studying, whether the class is held face-to-face or online. She suggests a preview-view-review approach. *Previewing* involves looking at the entire course before beginning it, including reading and reviewing the syllabus and planning ahead for assignments, papers, exams, and any scheduled chat sessions. *Viewing* means actually doing the work of the course and keeping up to date with it. *Reviewing* occurs once the course has begun. It involves looking back over discussion postings and other materials in order to prepare for exams and quizzes, writing papers, engaging in collaborative small group activities, and reflecting on the knowledge gained and learning that has already occurred. In order to review, students must make sure they have all the materials and notes they need, which is easier to do online because most course material is available on the course website throughout the term.

In any class, it may be easy for students to cut corners and accomplish only the very basics needed to complete the course. But Gilbert notes that in order to gain deep learning from an online course, students must also focus on the meaning of what the instructor is offering or has created, connect the new ideas generated to previous knowledge, and relate the class facts and information to real-life experience. In this way, students will be engaging in the reflective, transformative practices that are the hallmark of online learning, and they are likely to become self-directed, critical thinkers in the process.

In order to achieve a reflective approach to online learning, the virtual student must set aside some time several times a week to focus on the class. Allowing only one day per week to read and complete assignments will not be enough; posting requirements average two to three times per week. Nor will they be able to respond adequately to the ideas of their peers and thus contribute to the overall learning of the group. The virtual student, then, needs to practice becoming efficient and effective in online work. Once again, this can be illustrated with a four-quadrant diagram, as shown in Figure 7.2.

Unimportant Things Done Poorly

If a student does unimportant things poorly, that indicates both low effectiveness and low efficiency. Rather than attending to unimportant things and then doing a poor job of them, the student should be encouraged to let the unimportant go altogether and focus on more important tasks.

FIGURE 7.2. BUDGETING TIME EFFICIENTLY AND EFFECTIVELY.

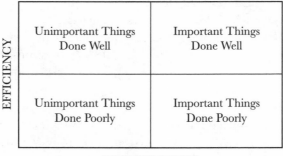

Important Things Done Poorly

If important things are done poorly, it indicates high effectiveness but low efficiency. The job is done, but so what? Often, when the student waits until the last minute to complete a task, this is the result. In our classes, we find that we need to return assignments for a second go-round in order to increase the level of efficiency. Unfortunately, we find that we are the exception and not the rule in this regard as students tell us they have never had this type of feedback before. Letting substandard work slide only increases the likelihood that virtual students will continue a pattern that does not serve their learning well. Just as in the face-to-face classroom, it is important to communicate in an online class that simply turning in assignments will not equate to a good grade in the course.

Unimportant Things Done Well

If a student does unimportant things well, it indicates low effectiveness but high efficiency. As with unimportant things done poorly, the question raised is "So what?" We have had students spend an inordinate amount of time on something that was completely irrelevant to the course and then proudly submit it to us, only to be shocked when we returned it as unacceptable. Again, making time for what is important can help a student avoid this pitfall.

Important Things Done Well

As with the previous figure, we hope that the virtual student will strive to work in this last quadrant, doing important things well. This indicates high effectiveness and high efficiency. When students effectively manage time and complete tasks efficiently, the likelihood that they will meet learning objectives, contribute to the learning of the learning community, and successfully complete the course greatly increases.

Once they learn to budget their time effectively, all of this is possible. Some students find that if they actually schedule periods for the various activities required of them in an online class, they will meet the goal of efficiency and effectiveness. Others find schedules too confining; they may use to-do lists where activities for the week are shown in order of priority. The trick is to keep the unimportant activities off the list completely so that when the important activities are done, time can be found for work on a project with a long deadline. Using schedules and lists can also help students avoid feeling overloaded because urgent but unimportant activities are given lower priority during the week, reducing feelings of stress and giving them a greater sense of control over the learning process.

Avoiding Overload

Time off should be included in the time budget for an online course. Because the online classroom is effectively open twenty-four hours a day, seven days a week, it is easy to spend too much time there, thus leading to feelings of overload. This is true not only for the virtual student but for the instructor as well. As we have gained more experience with online teaching we have come to the conclusion that building in time off is a good practice. Capella University, with which we are affiliated, builds a break week into all of its online classes. At first we were surprised and put off by this practice, but we have come to value it. Break week is a time to get caught up with postings and assignments. It is a good way to create "breathing room" in what is otherwise a very intensive process.

We recommend that both faculty and students build in weekly time off too. For example, instructors may notify students that they will not check into the course on Saturdays, or even all weekend, depending on their own home demands. It is not unreasonable to indicate that no response will be made to e-mail on the weekends either. As long as students are notified in advance that the instructor will not be available at certain times, there should be no problem with this practice. Students may then create their own time-off schedules accordingly.

Both students and faculty who take or teach online courses recognize that working in this manner allows time for travel. Although we are not suggesting that either faculty or students schedule vacations in the middle of the term, being able to build in time for work-related travel is one of the benefits of working online. Consequently, if a guideline states that either students or the instructor can notify others of an unavoidable absence, the absence can be accommodated and the sense of an ongoing learning community preserved.

Overload can be significant in online learning. Because "students report information overload, communication anxiety, in relation to the delayed responses in an asynchronous environment, increased work and responsibility, difficulty in navigating online and following the discussion threads" (Harasim, Hiltz, Teles, and Turoff, 1996, p. 15), other ways to avoid overload should be suggested. Something that contributes to overload is the tendency of some instructors, particularly instructors new to the online environment, to include too much material for the time allotted to a course. The pace of an online course is slower; it takes longer to explore various topics through asynchronous discussion than it might in a face-to-face lecture or classroom discussion. Furthermore, in an online course students are expected to embark on a journey of discovery to seek out material related to course content and then bring that material back to the group. Therefore, the instructor needs only to provide enough material to set the stage; students will then do the rest. In this context, the following suggestions may help students avoid overload:

- Log on to the course site with the intention of downloading and reading only.
- Print new messages, if possible, to allow time to review them in a more leisurely fashion.
- Once messages have been read and reviewed, formulate a response to be posted. Do not feel an immediate response is necessary in an asynchronous environment.
- In order to be more thoughtful about responses, prepare them in a word processor and then copy and paste them to the course site. If hard disk space is at a premium or if a lab computer is being used, copy responses to a floppy disk and upload from there. (Palloff and Pratt, 1999, p. 53)

Minimizing the use of chat, or synchronous discussions, is another way to reduce overload. The scheduling concerns involved in setting up a time for a chat session, coupled with the intensity of sessions that involve more than just a couple of students, can create a significant degree of anxiety. Chat is best used with very small numbers of students for work on collaborative assignments, to accompany a whiteboard session, or during instructor office hours. It is also helpful to allow students to opt in or out of chat sessions. Finally, if it is possible to archive a chat session and make it available to students who are unable to attend, they will not miss out on what they might consider to be important information delivered at a time that is inconvenient for them. It is advisable to consider multiple means for delivering information contained in synchronous sessions.

How to Get Commitment and Buy-In

As we said in the previous chapter, time management skills should be discussed during an orientation to the online program. However, because many institutions do not yet offer orientation programs this task often falls to the instructor or to an adviser after the virtual student begins to struggle with time commitments. There are some proactive things that instructors can do at the beginning of an online course both to cover time management issues and to gain commitment and buy-in to the process of online learning.

We believe that the first week of an online course should be used for community-building activities, such as posting introductions or bios, discussing learning objectives, and discussing course guidelines. This sets the stage for the online course itself, gives students a preview of what is to come during the term, and helps them develop realistic expectations of the amount of time they will need to commit to the course. Using a "syllabus scavenger hunt," where students are asked to find various elements or items and report back when they do, is a creative way to accomplish this process. Some instructors use a syllabus quiz, which counts for a small portion of the grade in the course. All of this is done to ensure that the students read and understand the syllabus and the course expectations. We often then ask our students either to send us an e-mail or to post a message to the discussion board noting that they have read and understood the syllabus and agree to the terms contained in it, such as the requirements for postings. This creates a contract for learning, which we can refer back to if problems come up down the line or if guidelines need to be renegotiated.

Some instructors have raised the concern that devoting the first week to community-building activities causes time crunches in already packed courses. However, if achievable learning objectives are established and a reasonable amount of material is contained in the course, and if there is an intent to empower students to explore the territory together, then the time devoted to community building is well spent. We often ask our students to begin reading for the second week's discussion during that first week and also ask them to link their personal introductions to the course content. For example, an introductory question in a course on social change might be this: "Introduce yourself to the group and tell us how you've experienced change in your life. What was the nature of the change you experienced and how did you deal with it?"

Concluding Thoughts

Making sure that students understand the demands of online learning and gaining their commitment to the process may not be the only determinant of success, but it is a step in the right direction for keeping students engaged and involved. Table 7.1 summarizes the elements of time management that are important for online learning along with instructional techniques for promoting good time management.

Once we engage students in the process and help them to manage it for themselves, our next concern is how to evaluate the outcomes, both for student performance and for the objectives of the course overall. How successful have students been in achieving their goals? How successful have we as faculty been in structuring a course that allows for goal achievement? We now turn our attention to these and other important questions as we discuss how to assess student work and evaluate online courses.

TABLE 7.1   TIME MANAGEMENT AND ONLINE LEARNING.

Time Management Concern	Techniques to Promote Time Management
Setting goals	• Help students gain clarity about their goals for online study by providing detailed information about the demands of the online course. • Encourage realistic and flexible goal setting. • Encourage goal setting that takes all courses into account and looks to program or degree completion.
Setting priorities	• Encourage students to preview, view, and review course materials in order to determine which elements and assignments are important. • Post reminders of due dates in the course far enough in advance so that students do not prepare assignments in an urgent fashion.
Budgeting time	• Provide students with a realistic estimate of how many hours per week the course is likely to take. • Encourage students to budget time daily for assignment preparation and online participation. • Encourage students to check the course site daily, if possible, to see what is new and to keep up with course material. • Encourage students to remain flexible and communicate with the group if life events intervene and interfere with participation. • Minimize the use of chat, or make chat sessions optional, in order to reduce time constraints.
Avoiding overload	• Model good time management by establishing time off as the instructor or facilitator, and encourage students to build time off into their weekly schedules. • Encourage students to download course materials to allow for reflection time. • Encourage students to wait twenty-four hours before responding to material on the discussion board to slow down the pace and help them feel more in charge of their time. • Intervene with students who post excessively or make lengthy posts to allow other voices to be heard and to reduce overload on other students.
Commitment and buy-in	• Use syllabus quizzes or other means to ensure that students have read and understood the syllabus. • Ask students to post a message to the discussion board indicating that they have read and understood the syllabus and are prepared to abide by the terms of the syllabus; this creates the contract for learning.

TABLE 7.1   (*CONTINUED*).

Time Management Concern	Techniques to Promote Time Management
	• During the first week of class, engage students in a discussion on the discussion board about course guidelines and learning objectives in order to gain consensus, commitment, and buy-in.

CHAPTER EIGHT

ASSESSMENT AND EVALUATION

In our work with faculty groups across the country, we find that one of the most pressing topics raised is assessment and evaluation. Because online courses are so heavily based in discussion, instructors wonder how to evaluate their students' contributions. There is also some concern about online courses being evaluated in the same way that face-to-face courses are—for the purposes of course development, program development, and instructor effectiveness. Instructors note, however, that the courses are significantly different. Consequently, their evaluation of online courses should also be different. In this chapter, we explore the issues involved in assessment of student performance, course evaluation, and the important topic of plagiarism and cheating.

Assessment of Student Performance

According to Morgan and O'Reilly (1999), the purpose of student assessment is to provide support and feedback to enhance ongoing learning and report on what students have already achieved. Angelo and Cross (1993) state that most instructors aspire to assess more than knowledge of the content area being taught. Instead, "they hope to use subject matter to teach students to think—that is, to develop higher-level cognitive skills: to solve problems, analyze arguments, synthesize information from different sources, and apply what they are learning to new and unfamiliar contexts" (p. 106). How to do that effectively becomes the primary concern of the instructor. Should tests and quizzes be used? If not, how else might student progress be assessed? How should grades be assigned to the discussion area of the course?

Angelo and Cross believe that in order for assessment to be effective, it must be embedded into the design of the course. They note that effective classroom assessment has a number of characteristics: it is learner-centered, teacher-directed, mutually beneficial, formative, context-specific, ongoing, and firmly rooted in good practice. Although they are discussing assessment techniques for the face-to-face classroom, these same principles apply to the online classroom. We will look at each one in relationship to online learning.

Learner-Centered

Since a well-designed online course should be focused and centered on the learner, it follows that student evaluation in that course should be the same. As Angelo and Cross state: "To improve learning, it may often be more effective to help students change their study habits or develop their metacognitive skills . . . than to change the instructor's teaching behavior. In the end, if they are to become independent, lifelong learners, students must learn to take full responsibility for their learning" (1993, p. 4). The reflective process that should be encouraged in an online course provides the basis for learner-centered assessment. Students should be given credit for self-reflection, and self-reflection should be incorporated into the design and expectations for the online course.

Teacher-Directed

Even though online teaching and learning is focused on the learner, the instructor decides what to assess, how to assess it, and how to respond to any evaluation material contained in the reflective material submitted by students. Information about assessment and evaluation should be provided in the course guidelines and communicated to students at the beginning of the course. Grading rubrics can be helpful in determining how reflective material will be assessed. Exhibit 8.1 shows a grading rubric developed by Debbie King of Sheridan College for the evaluation of the discussion component of her course. This rubric gives clear direction to students and also reduces or eliminates any disagreements about grading at the end of the course. Additional examples of grading rubrics can be found in the faculty toolkit at the back of this book.

EXHIBIT 8.1.   SAMPLE GRADING RUBRIC FOR ONLINE DISCUSSION.

Score	Level of Participation During One Week
0 points	Minimum number of postings not met
7 points	Minimums met; all discussion on Level I
8 points	Minimums met; at least one example of discussion above Level I
9 points	Minimums met; at least one example of discussion above Level I with at least one above Level II
10 points	Minimums met; at least two examples of discussion above Level I with at least one above Level III

Evaluation of Levels of Thinking in Weekly Threaded Discussions

Critical thinking	Level I	Elementary clarification	Introduce a problem; pose a question; pass on information without elaboration.
	Level II	In-depth clarification	Analyze a problem; identify assumptions.
	Level III	Inference	Make conclusions based on evidence from prior statements; generalizing.
	Level IV	Judgment	Express an opinion about a conclusion or the relevance of an argument, theory, or solution.
	Level V	Strategy	Propose a solution; outline requirements for its implementation.
Information processing	Level I	Surface	Repeat information; make a statement without justification; suggest a solution without explanation.
	Level II	In-depth	Bring in new information; show links, propose a solution with explanation; show evidence of justification; present a wider view.
Skills	Level I	Evaluation	Question your ideas or approach to a task; for example, "I don't understand . . . "
	Level II	Planning	Show evidence of organizing steps needed and prediction of what is likely to happen;

EXHIBIT 8.1. (*CONTINUED*).

		for example, "I think I should . . . "
Level III	Regulation	Show evidence of implementing a strategy and assessing progress; for example, "I have done. . . . "
Level IV	Self-awareness	For example, "I believe. . . . " or "I have found. . . . "

Mutually Beneficial

Angelo and Cross state, "By cooperating in assessment, students reinforce their grasp of the course content and strengthen their own skills at self-assessment" (1993, pp. 4–5). If they collaboratively assess their progress and the course itself, students come to believe in the basic tenets of a learning community—they find themselves involved in something that is greater than the sum of its parts. They not only are engaged in a learning process but also have the ability to improve that process for themselves and others through feedback to the instructor. In so doing, they increase their ability to reflect and provide good feedback.

Formative

When they participate in assessment and provide reflection and feedback throughout the course, students are co-creating the course to meet their learning needs. Feedback received by the instructor should be carefully considered and alterations to the course should be made as the course progresses if the students feel that doing so would be beneficial and if it will improve their chances of achieving their learning objectives. For example, we recently conducted an online faculty development seminar in which the participants felt that the amount of time allowed for each unit of the course was simply not sufficient to complete the assignments. They requested that they be allowed ten days instead of seven to complete each unit. We made the modification, and because we were not operating in the framework of a traditional quarter or semester, adjusted the end date of the course as well. The participants were grateful for the extra time, felt heard by us, and also felt that they had had a hand in co-creating their learning process.

Context-Specific

What works well in one online course may not work well in another. For example, in a skill-based course, such as accounting or other math or science course, it may be necessary to use tests and quizzes to determine the degree to which students are acquiring the skills and knowledge contained in the course. In a more discussion-based course, such as organizational behavior or other courses in the social and behavioral sciences, tests and quizzes may not be the best assessment tool to use. Papers and evaluation of discussion material may be more appropriate in this case. Furthermore, because groups of students differ, it is necessary to be flexible. An instructor may decide to add quizzes if discussion is lagging in a course, making it difficult to assess where students are in their learning process. In sum, student assessment in a given course should be responsive to the needs and characteristics of the students, the instructor, and the subject matter being studied.

Ongoing

Meaningful assessment in the online course begins at the start of the course and continues throughout the process. When students post their introductions and learning objectives, they receive feedback both from the instructor and their peers, and this is the beginning of the evaluative practice that continues throughout the course. Including an area in the course for reflection assists with the evaluation process; so does a more structured midterm evaluation. Consider the following student comment taken from one course's reflections area, which comprised the midterm evaluation of an online course:

I think we are on target with our syllabus. I have enjoyed the discussions and we are getting to the meat of Electronic Learning Communities. One of the things that I have consistently experienced with my courses is being left with the nagging feeling that I really don't know what I know, if that makes sense. I mean we talked about what is an electronic learning community and I have some ideas, but there seems to be so much stuff out there like electronic community, e-learning, electronic learning community that I am still not satisfied I have gotten clear in my head about what is the difference? When I go to these websites, everything is referred to as electronic learning community, but it doesn't fit the description of what we are talking about. It is as if the term is so misused that people can call anything electronic learning community, but no one ever defines what they are talking about when they use the term and it is often very different meanings that people are applying. . . . I was under the impression, I just wasn't getting it, but when I started visiting all the sites that were called ELC, and when I saw how they described themselves, it was clear to me that each one had a different take on ELC. Anyway, ELC seems to be like so many other new concepts, it is evolving. *Cheryl*

Cheryl's comments initially indicated that she thought the course was on target, but by asking her for midterm feedback, she also was able to surface and get feedback on concepts that remained hazy to her. Thus, the assessment process helped to reinforce for her that she was understanding more than she expected and was moving in the direction of her learning objectives.

Firmly Rooted in Good Practice

The issue of best practice is often discussed by faculty in relationship to online teaching. We believe that instructors need to take their best teaching practices out of the face-to-face classroom and use them online, and we also believe that good assessment practice is part of good teaching practice. When constructing the assessment and evaluation components of an online course, an instructor needs to look at what has worked well face-to-face. Have tests and quizzes been an effective evaluation tool of students in the face-to-face realm? If so, how can those best be delivered in the online environment? Do papers and collaborative assignments make more sense? If so, then the assessment of papers and collaborative work should form the basis of student evaluation. Regardless of what is chosen, if the assessment is well-designed, clear, and easy for students to understand and relate to, it should work well online.

Morgan and O'Reilly (1999) describe six key qualities of assessment of online students: a clear rationale and consistent pedagogical approach; explicit values, aims, criteria, and standards; authentic and holistic tasks; a facilitative degree of structure; sufficient and timely formative assessment; and awareness of the learning context and perceptions. Put more simply, if the course is designed with clear guidelines and objectives, if tasks and assignments are relevant not only to the subject matter but to the students' lives as well, and if students understand what is expected of them, then assessment will be in alignment with the course as a whole and not be seen as a separate and cumbersome task. When the course and assessment techniques are aligned, then instructors and students alike are more satisfied with the outcome of the learning process. When that does not occur, students may become frustrated. The following example will help illustrate this idea.

One of us was teaching an online course in social psychology that was designed by another instructor. The course was fairly well designed, including good discussion questions that yielded active discussion, and written assignments that asked students to draw on relevant experiences from their lives in order to understand the key concepts of the course. The disconnect came when the students were required to sit for a proctored exam, which was not aligned with the way the course had been conducted yet counted for 50 percent of the grade. In the exam, students were asked to recall picky details from their reading assignments in the form of multiple-choice questions and to define terms. The students, most of whom had done well in the discussions and written assignments, did poorly on the exam. When the issue was raised with her, the department chair responded that the exam was the only way to be assured that the students had done their own work throughout the course. She did not feel comfortable with the notion that the ongoing, formative assessment of students had more weight and was perhaps more relevant. As a result, the students were frustrated and unhappy with their grades. They felt that the exam was not aligned with the course in any way.

It is important to balance the needs of students, the instructor, and the administration in creating assessment that is aligned with the learning objectives and teaching methods of the course. In this particular situation, including quizzes in the same format as the final exam might have better prepared students for what was coming later. Or the final exam might have been restructured as an essay test, which would have more closely paralleled the types of assignments the students completed during the term. Weimer (2002) notes that there are a series of activities that can enhance the learning potential of an exam, such as including short activities in the course that promote review of learning, asking students to summarize the course content on a regular basis as part of ongoing class discussion, or asking students to generate one potential test question for each content module and then using that bank of questions to create the final exam. Learner-focused assessment means inviting the learners to participate in the ways in which assessment is constructed. This applies as much to exams as to other means of student assessment in a course.

Morgan and O'Reilly's contention that assessment should be authentic and relevant as well as aligned with course objectives is a critical factor to consider when designing student assessment. Table 8.1, taken from an instructor's undergraduate course in organizational behavior, is a good example of one way to align learning objectives with assessment. What is most interesting is the variety of assessment techniques used to evaluate student progress in the course.

Byers (2002) notes that taking an interactive approach to assessment creates a process that is both formative and summative. An interactive approach includes the instructor's perception, the student's perception, and the student's performance. Tests and quizzes do not necessarily provide an interactive approach to assessment and may, in fact, raise anxiety to the point that learning does not occur. Often, institutional policy dictates the use of exams, which is a challenge for instructors who choose a more interactive approach. Nevertheless, a final exam can be a good assessment as long as it connects to the course in a meaningful way. Other ways to assess online students include

- Tests and quizzes
- Self-assessments
- Peer assessments, including collaborative assessment
- Written reflections on the course, assignments, and overall learning

TABLE 8.1.   ALIGNING LEARNING OBJECTIVES WITH ASSESSMENT.

Learning Objective	Assessment
Understanding and application of organizational behavior concepts	Class discussions, experiential activities
Organizational analysis and problem solving	Analysis of case study provided by instructor, completion of original case analysis
Understanding of interpersonal and group interaction	Experiential activities, class discussions
Mastery of organizational behavior vocabulary and theoretical concepts	Exams, quizzes, class discussions, final paper
Application of technology in learning, research, and problem solving	Internet usage, electronic submission of assignments, e-mail, participation in chat sessions

- Projects, papers, and collaborative group assignments
- Critical evaluation of contributions to the discussion board
- Journals and portfolios

In sum, how assessment occurs is not as important as how relevant it is to the course content and learning objectives.

Course Evaluation

Angelo and Cross (1993) suggest that instructors ask themselves three critical questions when trying to develop good course evaluation: What are the essential skills and knowledge I am trying to teach? How can I find out whether students are learning them? How can I help students learn better?

Just as student evaluation must be aligned with learning objectives and be an ongoing process throughout the course, so should course evaluation.

Faculty are concerned that traditional course evaluation methods do not adequately measure the effectiveness of their online instruction and courses. Brookfield (1995) notes that traditional course evaluation rarely measures what we want it to measure. Instead of looking at whether the course, as it was designed, supported students in achieving learning objectives, evaluations tend to measure how well the students liked the instructor as a presenter—in other words, course evaluation is something of a popularity contest.

But in online learning—where it is important to look at a number of issues, including course design, the technology in use, and whether a learning community formed to support learning—traditional course evaluation is fairly useless. The instructor in the course is represented by words on a screen, so the tendency for course evaluation to be a kind of popularity contest is somewhat diminished. Still, students will evaluate the instructor's presence in and engagement with the course, as demonstrated by the number and quality of instructor posts, responsiveness to questions, and support and assistance with projects, papers, and assignments. Therefore, online instructors would do well to model the type of behavior they want to see in their students—and then evaluate how well they did that.

Formative evaluation, which is ongoing throughout a class, is more helpful in evaluating its effectiveness than the traditional summative evaluation given at the end of the class. Summative evaluation should not be abandoned, but it also should not be used as the only measure of effectiveness. We find that when a solid learning community has been developed, students are more willing to be honest about their experience in the course and will share their feelings openly with the instructor. We are rarely surprised by the results of the anonymous summative evaluations we receive at the end of our online courses because of the formative evaluation we encourage as the course is in session. Here are some evaluative comments offered by students in one of our online courses on social change:

I have to say that at first I found this class a little difficult. I had a hard time understanding the reading. But I soon realized that when I combined the reading with my classmates' and instructors' comments, I was able to grasp a much better understanding of the concepts. I learned the most from the course room interaction. The knowledge, insights, and feedback from everyone is priceless. I enjoyed learning about everyone's different experiences and ideas. Although the material was difficult and not my favorite topic (to be honest) the in-class experiences made this class valuable. *Teri*

I have come to appreciate that the world is a difficult place to understand. The solutions seemed much simpler before I took this course. The movement towards liberal democracy and capitalism was not as well understood before I took this course. The constancy of change is even more clear, as well as the resistance to it. We have often referred to the events of 9-11 and the situations since, and the resistance to change— It isn't the way it's supposed to be. Things aren't supposed to change. Change is scary and frightening. But, as we have seen, if you do not change, you become extinct. The world is changing and will continue to change. Hanging onto the past, making judgments about who's right or wrong or who's entitled to whose cheese is a way of resisting and avoiding change. We as a world are on a clear course towards a global community, global economy and global culture. As it grows, the people who resist change will object, and even fight to try to prevent this unstoppable trend from occurring. This is my greatest learning. Thank you for your leadership and guidance. It's been a pleasure and fun with the discussions. *Mike*

These students' comments indicate achievement of learning objectives rather than how much they liked or did not like the instructor. As a result, they are much more helpful when instructors think about future delivery of the course.

One technique for summative evaluation of a course, suggested by Brookfield (1995), is to have students write a letter to those students who will follow them in future offerings of the course. Brookfield suggests that these letters be collected by a group reporter and then that aggregated data from the letters be shared with the class and the instructor. But we have found that in the online learning community, because of the relative anonymity of the medium, students are willing to share their letters directly with one another and the instructor. We also like to give credit, but not a grade, for turning in the letter. For example, the letter or a final reflections piece might be worth ten points in the total points allotted for the course. We have adapted Brookfield's directions for writing the letter as follows:

Writing a Letter to Successors:

In this exercise, we'd like you to write a letter to be sent to new students who will take this online course after you do. What we'd like you to tell them as specifically as you can is what you think they should know about to survive and flourish in this class. Some themes you might consider are:

• What you know now that you wish you had known at the beginning of this class
• The most important thing to do in order to keep your sanity as you take this class
• The most common mistakes that you made and saw others make in this class
• Any advice you have on how to make it through this class successfully

These themes are to guide you—you may ignore them or use them as you see fit. After you have written your letter, you can either post it in the Electronic Reflections section of the course or send it to me via e-mail.

Most institutions require some form of summative evaluation at the close of a course. It is important to create an evaluation that reflects the nature of online learning and is not a replica of evaluation forms used in face-to-face classrooms. An anonymous summative evaluation should cover the following elements:

• The overall online course experience
• Orientation to the course and course materials
• The content, including quantity of material presented and quality of presentation

- Discussion with other students and the instructor
- Self-assessment of level of participation and performance in the course
- The courseware in use; ease of use and ability to support learning in this course
- Technical support
- Access to resources

Including all of these elements in a summative evaluation takes it to a new level. It is no longer focused solely on how well the instructor may or may not have performed but also looks at the total experience the virtual student had with the course. Just as with the development and teaching of online courses, institutions need to think creatively when they evaluate those experiences.

A Few Words About Plagiarism and Cheating

Because the instructor does not control the learning process in online learning and because of the inability to physically see the learners in online courses, it has been assumed that plagiarism and cheating occur more frequently in this medium. Morgan and O'Reilly (1999) note that some institutions have adopted surveillance methods to authenticate virtual student identity during exams, such as the use of desktop cameras and retina scanners. However, they believe that these techniques reflect institutional thinking that students are "born cheats." Morgan and O'Reilly state, "In open and distance contexts, most learners are adults who are not interested in cheating or taking the work of another" (1999, p. 96). This may be a fairly optimistic view, because cheating and plagiarism do happen online. According to recent studies, plagiarism and cheating occur about as frequently online as they do in face-to-face classes (Kellogg, 2002).

Even if cheating and plagiarism do not occur as frequently as we may think, that is no reason to ignore the possibility. It is far more effective to take proactive steps to avoid cheating and plagiarism than to deny the possibility or to overreact and alienate students through a lack of trust.

When a course is well-constructed and learner- and community-centered, and promotes empowerment and reflection, the issue of cheating should diminish. Furthermore, including assignments that promote critical thinking skills and collaboration, rather than individualism and competition, will also help reduce the temptation to cheat. In collaborative learning environments, students are not only cheating themselves but cheating the group if they plagiarize or take the work of another.

However, some precautions that instructors can take to further reduce the presence of cheating or plagiarism in their courses are as follows:

- Be alert to changes in student behavior or differences in writing style in posts to the discussion board and assignments. Students develop a signature way of posting. If their assignments differ significantly from that, then an examination of why that occurred may be necessary.

- Modify discussion questions and assignments used in a course with some frequency. This reduces the possibility that a student may be able to use a roommate's discussion responses, for example, or the same paper that another student has written. In addition, instructors need to be aware of similarities in writing and postings and question the student if a familiar piece of writing shows up a second time.

- Harris (2002) notes, "In my experience, other than the whole-paper or paragraph-after-paragraph type of plagiarism, most plagiarism occurs through the student's lack of understanding about how to quote, paraphrase, and cite sources. Many students simply do not know what they are doing" (Final Advice to Instructors, ¶ 1). Therefore, it is helpful to provide a thorough explanation of what constitutes plagiarism and the importance of citing the work of another, even to the extent of giving other students credit for ideas used. We frequently ask students to use citations from the reading in their discussion posts and inform them that the presence of citations will be evaluated.

- When tests or quizzes are used, administer them in a proctored environment or embed questions of a personal nature in them that only the particular student would be able to answer. For example, early in the course, an instructor may ask students to provide personal information, such as the color of their mother's or father's eyes, and then ask for that information somewhere in a test. This method is not foolproof, however. There are no good safeguards, other than proctoring, that are currently available to ensure that the people taking the exam in the online environment are the students enrolled in the course.

- Consider including process steps when students are completing papers, with pieces of the work turned in at varying points throughout the term.

- Require the use of recent sources; many papers that are copied or available for purchase are out of date and use old sources.

- Check sources, particularly Internet sources, and if you have serious concerns about the possibility of plagiarism, ask students to submit copies of their sources along with their papers.

- When all else fails, and plagiarism is suspected, use a service such as TurnItIn.com or Plagiarism.com to determine to what degree the paper was lifted from another without proper citation. The report generated by the service used will provide information needed to counsel the student or take disciplinary action, whichever is called for by institutional policy.

Once again, a collaborative approach that stresses the formation of a learning community is the best defense against plagiarism and cheating.

Concluding Thoughts

Byers (2002) states, "The learner-centered environment is widely accepted as the optimum educational paradigm. This paradigm implies that the students themselves are the primary learning resource, which means that the instructor, as the designer of the learning environment, must sincerely and proactively discern the students' needs and opinions about their learning, respond in a timely and effective fashion, and constantly inform the students about what actions are being taken and why. . . . Applying these data course changes while the course is ongoing demonstrates to the students that their feedback has an effect, and makes manifest that their learning is a cooperative effort by themselves and their instructor" (Conclusion section, ¶ 2). The more we engage our students in an ongoing evaluation of their own performance and of the course, the more meaningful the course will be to them and the more likely it is that we will develop empowered and lifelong learners. A summary of our suggestions for embedding assessment and evaluation in an online course is shown in Table 8.2.

The topic of plagiarism and cheating lends itself to further investigation. How do instructors help students understand what plagiarism is? How can we also teach them about issues of copyright as they apply to student work? We will now focus on these questions as we look at the legal issues that both virtual students and their instructors face.

TABLE 8.2. SUGGESTIONS FOR EMBEDDING ASSESSMENT AND EVALUATION INTO AN ONLINE COURSE.

Evaluation-Assessment Concern	Evaluation-Assessment Techniques
Student assessment	• Design learner-centered assessments that include self-reflection. • Design and include grading rubrics for the assessment of contributions to the discussion as well as written assignments. • Include collaborative assessments through public posting of papers along with comments from student to student. • Encourage students to develop skills in providing feedback by providing guidelines to good feedback and modeling what is expected.

TABLE 8.2. (*CONTINUED*).

Evaluation-Assessment Concern	Evaluation-Assessment Techniques
	• Use assessment techniques that fit the context and align with learning objectives. • Design assessments that are clear, easy to understand, and likely to work in the online environment. • Ask for and incorporate student input into how assessment should be conducted.
Course evaluation	• Embed evaluation in the course, make it ongoing throughout the course. • Provide an area on the course site designated for evaluation and reflection. • Consider using creative means of course evaluation, such as letters to successors, and give credit for completing evaluations. • Include both formative and summative evaluation in the course. • Design summative evaluations that go beyond commenting on the instructor, but include evaluation of the learning experience, technical support, and the technology in use.
Plagiarism and cheating	• Use a variety of assessment techniques, including tests and quizzes, journals, collaborative assignments, papers and projects, and others. • Be alert to changes in student posting and assignment style. • Modify discussion questions and assignments each term that the course is offered. • Use process steps in completing assignments. • Minimize the use of individual, competitive situations and maximize the use of collaboration and community building. • Check sources cited in student work. • Use proctoring for exams. • Teach about what constitutes plagiarism. • If all else fails, use a plagiarism detection service.

CHAPTER NINE

LEGAL ISSUES AND THE VIRTUAL STUDENT

Although much has been written and continues to be written on faculty concerns about intellectual property and copyright, little to no attention has been paid to how these issues affect the virtual student. When students participate in an online course, they are, in fact, co-creating a text on the topic along with their instructor and their peers. Despite this, students are rarely asked for their consent for their contributions to be archived with the course on the university's server. In addition, students may make original contributions to the course in the form of papers, projects, or reference materials that may be incorporated into course revisions. Again, rarely are students asked for their consent, nor are any arrangements made with them to compensate them for their contributions—it is assumed that this is part and parcel of participation in an online course. In this chapter, we focus on these issues and discuss the following questions:

- Who owns a student's work once it is posted to a discussion board?
- What privacy issues need attention in an online course?
- How do we deal with the archiving of courses and use of those courses later on?
- How do intellectual property and copyright issues affect students?
- What are some of the legal issues and trends?
- What do the experts say about these issues?
- What do we recommend faculty and administrators do when it comes to legal issues and online classes?

Who Owns My Work?

For the last few years, faculty have been engaging in discussions with their institutions about course ownership and intellectual property rights as they concern online courses. The American Association of University Professors (1999), in its statement on intellectual property and distance education, states that online education "invariably presents administrative, technical, and legal problems usually not encountered in the face-to-face classroom" (p. 41). As a result, institutions are revisiting their policies on intellectual property to define what it is, author rights when developing online courses, how online courses developed by faculty can be used, how faculty will be compensated for the development of these courses, and who will be responsible and liable for administering intellectual property policies. However, when it comes to students, little to no attention is being paid to these issues except as regards the handling of copyright infringements by students. Where, then, will the appropriate policies come from?

The American Council on Education (2000) has addressed this issue but has not offered policy suggestions for dealing with it. The council suggests, however, that this is a student privacy issue and notes that some institutions have requested that students participating in a distance education program execute a release or waiver that permits the use of their image or online contributions to the discussion board. Constance Hawke (2001) discusses student privacy issues and states that although the U.S. Department of Education has used a broad interpretation of what constitutes a private educational record under the Family Educational Rights and Privacy Act (FERPA), some courts have taken a much more restrictive view. She notes that thus far the issue has been addressed with regard to disciplinary records but has not been raised regarding computer records maintained by the university. We wonder, then, if simply getting a waiver to reuse or store material at the beginning of a course is enough.

Students make significant contributions to the process of online learning and to course development, so is obtaining a blanket release enough to protect their rights? We believe that students have the right to know how courses will be archived, who will have access to that archive, the purpose for which the material will be used, and how long that course archive will be kept. These are questions that we have been asked by students and strongly suspect have been asked of other faculty as well. We have rarely had students object to the archiving of their contributions to the discussion along with the course. However, it does happen, and students should be given the opportunity to remove any photos or graphic representations they may have posted along with their contributions to discussions before archiving if they so choose.

If students make substantive contributions to the development or revision of an online course, such as by providing papers used as supplemental reading material or models used to support the learning of successors, then more specific consent arrangements need to be in place and royalty and compensation schemes need to be considered. For example, we teach a master's project course online. We have been asked periodically to select examples of exceptional work to be used as models for other students and to be showcased by the institution. We ask for and receive the consent of the student or do not use the work in this way. We find that most students are honored by the request and gladly give consent without asking for any form of compensation. However, we would never consider using their work in this way without first asking.

Another related issue is whether a formal consent form should be signed or whether a student can give consent via e-mail. In our experience, students seem more willing to respond to an e-mail request and are less likely to return a form through the postal service. Whether an e-mail consent is considered a legal consent is not clearly defined, however. Consequently, using both e-mail and a formal comment form that is signed and returned by mail is likely to cover more bases legally.

Can I Say What I Really Want To?

Privacy concerns as well as issues of freedom of speech may also extend to what is said in the online classroom. For the most part, we encourage our students to express themselves freely, even if their opinions are controversial. However, because online courses are private and password-protected, some limits must be established and maintained, including these:

- *Harassment:* Hawke (2001) notes, "Conflict may arise when electronic 'speech,' which is not proscribable, nevertheless creates a hostile or offensive environment for a particular class of users. Internet speech can be discriminatory on ethnic, racial, or religious grounds; however, in light of the proliferation of sexual material available, a dominant concern appears to be sexual harassment" (p. 63). In creating guidelines for an online course, an instructor may wish to include specific information about what constitutes harassment or discrimination, make it clear that harassment or discrimination will not be tolerated, and describe the action that will be taken if such behavior occurs. Harassment is not limited to the discussion board of the online classroom. Stalking and harassment have occurred through e-mail. If a student reports that he or she is being stalked by a classmate, swift action must be taken in order not only to protect the student being stalked but to preserve the safety of the learning community.

- *Pornography:* Students have been known to upload pornographic material in graphics or text to an online course. When this occurs, the instructor needs, once again, to work swiftly to remove the material. The student should be contacted immediately and told to remove it. If he or she refuses, the instructor should do so and consider further disciplinary action, such as removing the student's password and access to the online course. Students need to know that including pornography in an online course is behavior that will not be tolerated.
- *Flaming:* Hawke notes that the courts define "fighting words" as communication that can create an *immediate* breach of the peace. To date, there has been no case law established with regard to the electronic environment and fighting words; the issue has only been related to face-to-face environments where a confrontation is the likely result. Those of us who teach online, however, know that flaming—an angry, personal attack—can have devastating results in an online class. When flaming occurs, students generally report feeling unsafe and insecure and that they can no longer express themselves freely for fear of retaliation. Although we are not aware of any face-to-face confrontations that have occurred as the result of a flaming incident online, the possibility certainly exists. Once again, the instructor needs to act quickly when flaming occurs, communicating with the student who is responsible and reminding him or her of the guideline for professional communication. If the issue cannot be resolved either outside or inside the online classroom, then the student should be removed and the others notified of the action taken.

Including material on the limits of communication in the guidelines for the course is one way to prevent inappropriate communications. Rather than seeming punitive, it can help to create a sense of safety and security that is needed for the development of a strong learning community. In our experience, we have only rarely had to invoke the sanctions we discuss with students. In addition, having students "sign off" on the guidelines—indicating that they have read and understood them and are willing to abide by them—helps tremendously if a student begins to stray from what is expected.

Use of Student Work in Faculty Research

Researching, writing, and publishing are significant parts of the work that faculty are normally required to do. Increasingly, faculty are writing about topics related to online learning, particularly as they gain experience with various aspects of working in this medium. As this occurs, the role of the virtual student in that research is increasing. Our own work is a point in fact. Clearly, we ask students to be an integral part of the work we do. How, then, should faculty include the virtual student in research without violating privacy rights?

When we do our own writing, we tend to review our courses to look for themes, issues, concerns, facts, researchable items, and new ideas that may not have occurred to us previously. And as we have done in this book, we like to use student posts to illustrate various points. We believe that our students not only have something significant to say but sometimes say it better than we can. Consequently, we are very careful about asking students for their permission to use their material in our work. Because we like to sign their posts with their first names, we also ask about that and give them the option of using an alias. Finally, to protect their privacy further, we remove any identifying information that might link them to a particular institution or workplace.

We have found our students to be extremely generous in giving their permission to be a part of our writing. However, some faculty have reported to us that, when they do other forms of research, students have been more reluctant to give consent for use of their material, to participate in surveys, or to contribute in some other significant ways. Other faculty have expressed confusion about the need to receive permission from students, especially when reporting aggregate outcomes of courses and the like.

Primo and Lesage (2001) state that the use of material posted to a listserv or discussion board must have the express permission of the individual and the group. It is simply good practice to contact students when research is to be done to notify them of the intent and to ask for consent to use material. Recently, we posted a request on the discussion board of an online course asking students if we might use material posted in the course. We told them they were free to say no. In so doing, we received both individual and group consent to use the material.

Some institutions ask for informed consent at the beginning of an online course or program not only to archive student contributions to the course itself but also so that the archives can be used in research after the course has ended. Such consents include a description of what the research is likely to be about and how individual privacy rights will be protected. Although this is a good practice, we still strongly believe that students or former students should be contacted individually when the research begins to ensure that they understand the nature of the research being conducted and to double-check on their willingness to participate. Our students are not words on a screen; they are people whose privacy and confidentiality need to be protected.

Training Students in Copyright and Intellectual Property Issues

Morgan and O'Reilly (1999) assert that most plagiarism occurs as a result of ignorance about the appropriate rules of citation and is not intentional. Because virtual students are working online and making greater use of the Internet as a research tool, confusion about how and when to cite increases. Primo and Lesage (2001) state, "With the explosion in the use of distance education, the amount of information and the degree of public access to it has grown exponentially. Increasing numbers of distance learning courses, especially on the Internet are redefining the boundaries of intellectual property" (New Challenges to Copyright Issues for Distance Learning, ¶ 1). Furthermore, each new version of the style manuals that students refer to in writing papers modifies its instructions for the citation of Internet-based material, adding to the confusion. Because Internet sites are so easy to access and often are not password-protected, students may mistakenly believe that all Internet sites are in the public domain and do not require citation. We have experienced two instances where students copied Internet sites almost completely in a paper and were quite upset to discover that this was considered plagiarism.

The issue is not limited to Internet sites, however. Often students will lift large sections of text from a book or journal article, give credit to the author, and be unaware that this is not acceptable practice. In fact, in some countries and cultures where copyright laws are not as stringent as in the United States, this practice is not considered plagiarism at all.

One effective means by which to reduce the possibility of plagiarism or copyright violations is to train students in the use of copyrighted material. Partnering with the institution's librarian to deliver this training can be helpful because librarians are generally fairly expert in these issues. Such training can and should be included in an online program or course orientation. However, some institutions are creating separate courses specifically to deal with issues of copyright and plagiarism. They offer them not only to their online students but also to their students taking classes face-to-face. Here are some important topics to cover during training:

- Definitions of copyright and fair use
- Avoiding plagiarism and copyright violations
- Search techniques
- Using electronic resources, such as databases and Internet sites
- Appropriate citation format for both electronic and print resources
- Evaluating websites and other electronic and print resources for inclusion in papers
- Validating the information found on websites
- Writing and formatting a research paper

Again, it is important to assume good intent—students are not "born cheats"; they usually plagiarize out of ignorance. Taking a proactive stance can reduce or eliminate problems before they begin and assist students in learning some important research skills along the way.

Making Students an Integral Part of the Process

Tony Bates (2000) suggests that students be made a part of task forces and committees charged with the planning of online courses and programs. By including students in the process, institutions make them an integral partner in the development of these courses and programs, and also educate them about the issues that the institution, the faculty, and their peers face in the development and delivery of online courses. And when students are included on task forces and committees, institutions are educated about the student role, view, and needs.

How does this affect discussions about copyright and intellectual property as they apply to the virtual student? Students need to be involved in the development of training programs on these issues as well as in the development of policy that responds to their needs, respects their privacy, and rewards their contributions to the online course development process should that occur.

Primo and Lesage (2001) note that institutions must facilitate the development of criteria for establishing ownership, future use, and distribution rights for material produced by faculty, students, and the institution. The virtual student cannot be ignored in this process because of the contribution he or she makes to the ongoing development of online courses. Primo and Lesage echo our own thoughts when they state that "legislation and accepted practice must change and adapt in order to make the most out of the possibilities of distance learning" (New Challenges, Few Answers, ¶ 1).

We cannot do business as usual in a medium that is unusual. Consequently, as we move forward in the development and delivery of more and more online classes and programs, the student's role in intellectual property and copyright issues must be given increasing consideration.

Concluding Thoughts

Clearly, the legal issues involved in online learning are arising as we go. No clear policies or regulations yet exist in this area. However, based on the existing literature, we believe the following:

- Online students own their own work. Therefore, they have the right to say how it will and will not be used.

- If students make a significant contribution to the course and it is incorporated into future iterations of that course, they need to be compensated in some fashion.
- Students need to be educated on issues of privacy, and their privacy needs must be respected.
- Students need training in fair use, copyright, and plagiarism to prevent inadvertent errors in any of these three areas.
- Institutions cannot remain passive on the legal issues involved with online learning. They must take a proactive stance in developing policies that are responsive to both student and faculty needs.
- The student viewpoint and voice must be included in the development of policies on these issues.

Table 9.1 summarizes the material covered in this chapter, the legal issues facing the virtual student and faculty, and institutional responses to those issues. Although some of these issues should be dealt with through institutional policy, a number of legal concerns can and should be addressed in the online classroom as well.

The next chapter in this guide to working with the virtual student focuses on issues of attrition, retention, and group size. How can we attract students to online courses and programs? What are the potential roadblocks to their success and how can faculty and institutions minimize those obstacles? In Chapter Ten we discuss these issues and make suggestions for minimizing attrition and maximizing success.

TABLE 9.1. ADDRESSING LEGAL CONCERNS IN THE ONLINE CLASSROOM.

Legal Issues in the Online Classroom	Techniques for Addressing Legal Issues
Ownership of material	• Provide an informed consent regarding ownership of course material and ask students to sign it at the beginning of an online course. • Any modifications to the consent should be addressed individually and at the time they occur—the initial signed consent should be appropriately modified as necessary. • Consider royalty or compensation to students when contributions to a course result in revisions or additions.

Privacy	• Educate students about acceptable and unacceptable behavior online. • Confront and intervene in all breaches of communication ethics or privacy immediately. • Cover privacy and communication concerns in course guidelines and ask students to sign off on the guidelines by posting a message of agreement to the course site.
Archiving courses	• Inform students about what course material will be archived and how that archive will be used. • Allow students sufficient time to remove material they consider to be personal, such as photos or graphic representations, before courses are archived. • Ask for consent to archive courses with student discussion intact. • If archived material is used later for the purpose of course revision or faculty research, ask students for consent to use material.
Using student work in faculty research	• Ask students for informed consent to participate in faculty research or if archived discussion is to be used. • If quotes are to be used, give students the option of using fictitious names. Remove any other identifying information, such as institutional or workplace affiliation.
Intellectual property and copyright	• Provide information or training to students on plagiarism and copyright. • Include in the training information on appropriate citation format and definitions of copyright and fair use. • Include students in policy development and the development of training programs to address legal issues and concerns.

CHAPTER TEN

ATTRITION, RETENTION, AND GROUP SIZE

Many critics of online education point to the higher dropout rates reported in these classes as a measure of their poor quality. As we mentioned earlier, online course attrition has been reported to be approximately 50 percent of those enrolled nationwide (Carr, 2000.) Diaz (2002) asserts that high dropout rates from online classes do not necessarily indicate either academic nonsuccess or poor quality. In fact Diaz states: "Online students often outperform traditional students when success is measured by the percentage of students that attain a grade of C or above, overall classroom performance (for example, exam scores), or student satisfaction" (Performance Differences, ¶ 1). So why do online students drop out of their classes at higher rates and what can be done to prevent the exodus? In this chapter, we explore some of the reasons for attrition from online courses as well as some steps to take to increase levels of retention. We close with our formula for quality in an online course because we believe that quality is the most important factor in determining whether a student will stay with an online course to completion.

Stopping the Exodus: Remembering What Students Need to Succeed

Much speculation has occurred about why students drop online classes more frequently than face-to-face classes. Diaz (2002) notes that there are many reasons why some students remain in online classes while others drop out. He includes student demographics as one reason, class quality as another, and the discipline of the course, socioeconomic factors, disabilities, and simple apathy as other reasons.

The demographics of the virtual student are widely confirmed: he or she tends to be older, working, and involved with family activities and the community. The convenience factor is what draws these students to the online environment, because it allows them the time for other equally important aspects of their lives.

We noted the characteristics of the successful virtual student early in this book. The virtual student:

- Has access to technology and computer skills
- Is open-minded about sharing personal details about his or her life, work, and other educational experiences
- Is not bothered by the absence of auditory and visual cues in the communication process
- Is willing to commit significant time to studies every week and does not see the course as the "softer, easier way"
- Can be developed into or already is a critical thinker
- Has the ability to reflect
- Believes that high-quality learning can happen anywhere, anytime

Let's now review each of these characteristics as it relates to retention in online courses and programs.

Access to Technology and the Skills to Use It

Clearly, students cannot be successful in an online class if their Internet access is shaky or nonexistent. We have had students drop our courses because their computer crashed and they were unable to find another way to complete the course. Technology can be a frustration to the virtual student; it can significantly hinder progress and become an obstacle that cannot be overcome. Furthermore, if a course is constructed in such a way that parts of it are not accessible to those on dial-up connections or those with disabilities, dropout rates may increase as students begin to see themselves falling behind. If a student encounters technical difficulties, it is important to let him or her know that other options for access exist, such as a computer lab on a local campus or in a public library. Although these options may be less convenient, they do allow students to continue with their coursework.

Open-Mindedness About Sharing Personal Details

If a student feels that personal boundaries are being crossed by the amount of shar-ing in an online course, he or she may pull back or drop out. As we have already stated, we do not expect an online course to turn into a therapy session for students, but a degree of openness is needed in order to humanize the environment and cre-ate a sense of connection. A level of sharing that is too intimate, however, can be-come uncomfortable for students who are unaccustomed to discussing personal details with others, either face-to-face or online. When a norm of intimacy is es-tablished in a group and one or more students are unable to comply with that norm, they may see dropping the course as their only option for dealing with the situa-tion. In this case, it is crucial for the instructor to intervene with these students and help them find a more comfortable way to interact in the course. The following student post indicates a level of discomfort with mandatory participation:

I personally enjoy reading fellow learner comments, but I generally don't respond to everyone unless there is something really striking that I want to comment on. Now if every learner thinks this way then there will not be a lot of chatter on the discussion link, but this would not make the learning community a failure. Of course if the in-structor demands that learners respond to every other learners comments (in other coursework this happened), then you will probably get comments, but maybe not heart-felt comments. . . . Take this course for example, I realize that the title is "Strate-gies For Building Online Learning Communities," but yet it is a course, and I as a learner am more interested in grasping concepts and developing comprehensive under-standing than I am in actually "being" in an online learning community. Of course if I stay up with the discussion questions then none of this matters. If I stay up, then I am a contributing member of the community without having to think about it. I hope this makes sense. *Jeff*

Jeff's comments indicate that he is experiencing some discomfort in partici-pation but has developed a way to cope: if he sticks to the discussion questions, he feels more comfortable with the process. His approach is certainly acceptable, be-cause students are not expected to bare their souls in an online class—they are simply expected to participate.

Ease with the Online Environment

A recent discussion in an online class illustrates the kind of discomfort with the absence of auditory and visual cues that some students may experience:

I was thinking twice before I had written my comments about the reading just for the very reason you mention about being in a PhD program. I think part of the chal-lenge is just not having a class to go to [in order] to specifically discuss difficult portions and having the opportunity to talk them through to understanding. I can look up terms, this is not difficult. I just need a way to make it real and if I think it is like some example I dream up, it would be nice to have validation or clarification. I just don't trust myself to be able to figure it all out accurately and I'd rather not wait until the paper gets graded to figure out that I had things all mixed up. *Kristine*

This style is a drawback to oral processors. I am more of an oral learner so I find myself wanting to be in the class to discuss for immediate clarification also. *Glen*

Helps in confidence level. I agree. We just have to pretend that the keyboard is our voice. *Nita*

These students, who are new to the process of online learning, are struggling to figure out how to overcome the absence of verbal and visual cues. But that they feel comfortable in discussing their discomfort and are supporting one another in dealing with it are positive signs. Students who "suffer in silence" over these issues, however, may not be able to overcome them and stay in the course.

Willingness to Commit the Necessary Time

Diaz (2002) states, "I believe that many online students who drop a class may do so because it is the *right thing to do*. In other words, because of the requirements of school, work, and/or family life in general, students can benefit more from a class if they take it when they have enough time to apply themselves to the class work. Thus, by dropping the class, they may be making a mature, well-informed decision that is consistent with a learner with significant academic and life experience" (Making Sense of Drop Rates, ¶ 1). In other words, as we have noted many times, the very elements that attract students to the online environment may cause them to drop out. This should not be considered a failure for either the student or the online program; rather, it is perhaps the best decision the student can make at the time. The timing of the drop, however, can be an issue—one that should be clearly explained to the student. For example, institutional deadlines and policies may affect them negatively, or there may be an impact on any small group projects they are a part of. Such factors should be explained to students so that they can make the best possible decision.

Critical Thinking Ability

The successful virtual student can work fairly independently, engaging with the course material with minimal intervention on the part of the instructor. The student who needs significantly more input from the instructor and is not willing or able to engage in collaborative discussion and activity with peers is less likely to do well online. Once this situation becomes apparent to a student, he or she may decide to withdraw from the course, or if course completion is achieved, may decide that online learning is not for him or her. Such a student is more likely to do better in a face-to-face classroom situation where group work is not an essential feature. Alerting students in advance to the paradigm shift that accompanies online teaching and learning may help to avoid this situation.

Reflective Ability

Just as critical thinking skills are important to success in an online class, the ability to reflect on the material presented by both the instructor and the student's peers will make or break a virtual student. Students need to value the contributions of their peers as highly as they do those of the instructor, and they need to be able to make sense of the material independently. Finally, they need to be able to capture and convey such reflections to the group. It is not uncommon for us to receive an e-mail or a phone call from students who feel that they simply cannot measure up to the class level. One of us had an experience with a student who needed to be away for several days without computer access. On her return, she was so overwhelmed by the quality and quantity of reflection among her peers that she began to question her own ability to contribute at the same level. After much discussion and soul searching, she decided to drop the course and take it in a face-to-face format, where she felt she could be successful. It seemed to us that this was one of the "mature decisions" to which Diaz refers.

Belief That High-Quality Learning Can Happen Anywhere and Anytime

We have mentioned often in this book that the successful virtual student does not believe the instructor is the fount of knowledge through which all learning flows but instead is flexible and open to learning in a new way. It is not uncommon to receive the following type of feedback from a student at the end of an online course: "But YOU didn't teach me." It is not likely that a student with this mindset will be successful online. Such students are at risk for dropping the class because they depend on the instructor, rather than the group, to generate knowledge in a course. Similarly, students who believe that quality learning only happens face-to-face will have a difficult time understanding the online learning process and may be disillusioned and dissatisfied with the experience.

Diaz creates three categories for all of the factors we have just reviewed: *student factors*, including educational preparation, motivation, and self-confidence; *situational factors*, such as family, work, and changes in personal and life circumstances;

and *educational system factors,* including the quality and difficulty of the course materials and the support provided by both the instructor and the institution.

Steps to Take to Improve Retention

Although quality is but one factor, it is an important one in retaining online students. Alley and Jansak (2001) note that there is no one agreed-upon checklist by which to rate course quality. Course quality is a relative concept that depends on who is judging it, course design, delivery of the course, and a host of uncontrollable factors that are likely to fall outside the pedagogical design of the course. Some of the external factors Alley and Jansak consider are those we have already discussed in this book:

- The fit between the course and the curriculum and the cohesiveness of the design of the course
- Students' ability to fit the course into the academic program and their lives
- Access to information and library services
- A sense of community
- Class or group size
- The technology used, and the technical support provided
- Learner characteristics, including learning style and lifestyle
- Instructor characteristics, including facilitation skills and presence

Institutions and instructors cannot ignore that there are factors that are out of our control that contribute to dropout rates in online courses. We can make inroads in some areas, but in others we will need future research to determine how to reduce the barriers to online learning and increase the likelihood of student success. Let us now look at those factors that we can influence along with some of the steps we can take to increase the likelihood of retention.

Ensure Greater Interactivity and Community Building

If we believe that knowledge is not transmitted but rather co-constructed, then it follows that the greater the interactivity in an online course and the more attention paid to developing a sense of community, the more likely students will stick with the course until its completion. No matter how difficult the material, if students believe that "we are all in this together," the possibility of retention increases because the feelings of isolation decrease. There is a sense that other people out there "understand." In fact, one of the criticisms leveled against online learning is what is perceived as an absence of personal interaction, which most students crave. We cannot emphasize enough that when the instructor is present—posting regularly to the discussion board, responding in a timely manner to e-mail and assignments, and generally modeling good online communication and interaction—students will do the same, and a high degree of interactivity will occur.

The instructor, then, should have three priorities in an online course: *promoting and developing a sense of community, keeping students engaged with the course and one another, and empowering students to take on and maintain the community-building process.*

A focus on these three elements helps students to believe that they are a part of a learning process that is bigger than their individual contributions to the course or their individual work on assignments. When the feeling of community is strong and interactivity is high, then students and instructors alike enjoy continuing the discussion online. Both groups will often comment on how much they look forward to logging on to see what might be new or in what directions the conversation has traveled. Furthermore, courses with high levels of interaction tend to get higher satisfaction ratings from students and show lower rates of attrition. Consequently, promoting a high level of interaction is a critical instructor role. In fact, it is probably the most important task an instructor can accomplish when teaching in the online environment.

If faculty are trained not just to deliver courses using technology but in pedagogical methods that lend themselves well to the online environment, and if developing community becomes a priority, the result can be a highly interactive course that leads to successful achievement of learning objectives and a sense of satisfaction for all concerned. Furthermore, when courses are designed and delivered with interactivity in mind, a shift occurs as learners become more empowered and discover that the learning in an online course comes from interacting with one another and not just with the instructor. When courses progress well, the instructor often learns as much from the students as the students learn from the instructor. This is one of the quality outcomes of participating in a learning community, and it is truly a learner-focused process.

Control Group Size

Another important factor over which institutions have some control, and that relates to the ability to develop community, is group size. Faculty often ask what the optimum number is for community building in an online course. As experienced online instructors, we feel that we can handle twenty to twenty-five students in an online course. Instructors who are new to the medium, or instructors teaching a course for the first time, should really teach no more than fifteen students. Unfortunately, this number sounds extremely low to many administrators who continue to believe that online learning will make significant amounts of money for the institution if the number of students enrolled in a course is high. But this is a serious error. As we have noted, students are seeking connection and a high degree of interaction with both instructors and their peers. When numbers in an online class are too high, they do not feel heard and may feel lost in the shuffle, just as they would in a large lecture class. Furthermore, as the numbers grow, the instructor's workload grows exponentially, causing increasing delays in response time to students and an inability to post to the discussion in a timely fashion. The result? Students may be less likely to stay with the course or to take another one in the future.

That said, instructors can deal with large numbers creatively by forming smaller discussion groups within the larger group of students in the class. Leadership for the discussion groups can be rotated, reporting out to the larger group on a regular basis—weekly, for example. Any synchronous chat sessions should be scheduled in such a way to minimize the number of students online at the same time; this holds true for both small and large groups of students. No more than ten to twelve students should be included in a synchronous session so that information overload and a sense of being overwhelmed, which can occur with large amounts of text scrolling rapidly on the screen, may be avoided.

Also, students in a large group situation should be clearly informed about what to expect from the instructor as far as response to postings, e-mail, and assignments. This can alleviate some of the frustration they may feel when the responsiveness is not as great as they wish. The instructor may also consider using synchronous online office hours as a means to increase the level of interaction with students in a large class.

Too small a group can also pose problems, however. A group must be large enough to have the critical mass that allows for interaction. In our experience, if there are fewer than five students in an online class the instructor needs to play a very active role in the group in order to keep participation alive.

Overall, however, although this makes us unpopular with administrators, we continue to believe that smaller is better in an online course. In addition to creating a more manageable workload for the instructor, smaller numbers support the community-building process, minimize information overload for all involved, and raise the perception of quality of the course as students feel recognized and heard.

Recognize That Not All Students (or Faculty) Belong in the Online Classroom

Diaz (2002) states, "Obviously, we should not neglect drop rates completely or avoid attempts to modulate the factors that lead to drops, but we should certainly not consider students who drop as 'at risk' students without further evidence to support such a belief" (Conclusions, ¶ 1). As we already noted, students who drop online courses may simply have made a decision that this environment is not for them and that the face-to-face environment serves their learning needs better. This does not put them in a high-risk category—there are many students who do well online, there are many students who do well face-to-face, and there are a number who do well with a blended approach. Going with a preferred learning style is certainly not a failure.

We strongly believe that it is a mistake to offer required courses only in online format, unless they are part of a completely online degree program or a program using a blended approach—a program that students choose to enter knowing that online courses are the main format. Similarly, we think it is a mistake to force instructors to teach online if they do not feel that the medium is right for them. Some degree of openness to teaching and learning online must be present for either instructors or students to be successful. At our seminars we have met some faculty who cannot see themselves moving their courses online and who are not open to doing so. They simply cannot rethink and reconfigure those courses for online delivery. In these cases, we have suggested using a web-enhanced or blended format, where face-to-face teaching is retained as the main mode of delivery while the instructor experiments with various online techniques, or that the instructor not go in the direction of online delivery at all.

There is no failure in a person admitting that he or she does not prefer the online environment, whether that person is an instructor or a student. However, once again, we offer a word of caution: it is important to allow students the opportunity to experience online learning if they are open to it. Using screening tools to screen out students may prevent students who could be developed into successful online learners from even getting started. At one of our recent seminars, an instructor informed the group that her institution had decided to use face-to-face interviews with students as a screening mechanism to determine who would be allowed to take online courses. Many instructors in the group found this approach problematic because, they felt, a face-to-face interview would not be a good indicator of online success. Learning through trial and error is a powerful way to learn. Consequently, we should not be afraid of letting students try. If we are creating high-quality, interactive courses, we can hope that students will at least be able to interact enough to complete the course and learn something in the process—even if what they learn is that online education is not for them.

Collaboration + Presence + Community = Quality

Earlier in this book we presented the features that virtual students are seeking when they sign up for an online course or program. They seek a program that is based on the ability to meet the unique educational needs, has a learner-centered rather than a faculty-centered focus, is cost-effective, has reliable technology that is easy to navigate and transparent to the user, and delivers appropriate levels of information and human interaction.

When instructors and students alike are able to reap the benefits of a well-designed online course and a responsive online degree program, the result is excitement about what is possible in the online realm and about the new relationships that are developed—between instructor and students, between students, and between instructor, students, and knowledge creation. This excitement about learning stimulates new, creative approaches to online teaching and learning and demonstrates that, in fact, high-quality, interactive courses are not just possible but already a reality. Figure 10.1 illustrates the elements that, we believe, form a high-quality online course or program that is truly learner-focused.

Table 10.1 summarizes the issues involved in the retention of the virtual student and techniques for improving retention.

FIGURE 10.1. ELEMENTS OF A HIGH-QUALITY ONLINE COURSE OR PROGRAM.

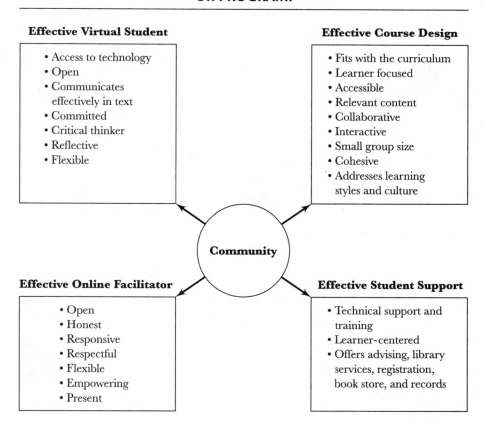

Effective Virtual Student

- Access to technology
- Open
- Communicates effectively in text
- Committed
- Critical thinker
- Reflective
- Flexible

Effective Course Design

- Fits with the curriculum
- Learner focused
- Accessible
- Relevant content
- Collaborative
- Interactive
- Small group size
- Cohesive
- Addresses learning styles and culture

Community

Effective Online Facilitator

- Open
- Honest
- Responsive
- Respectful
- Flexible
- Empowering
- Present

Effective Student Support

- Technical support and training
- Learner-centered
- Offers advising, library services, registration, book store, and records

Keeping an eye to quality, in the next chapter we will take a final look at virtual students as they experience online learning today as well as what their future concerns may be. In addition, we explore best practices in teaching in the online environment.

TABLE 10.1. IMPROVING QUALITY AND INCREASING RETENTION ONLINE.

Issues in Increasing Retention and Improving Quality	Techniques for Increasing Retention and Improving Quality
Reducing attrition	• Improve possibility of access by using simple course design, and encourage access through public sources, such as libraries and computer labs, if need be. • Intervene with students who are having difficulty with online communication to help them develop techniques that feel comfortable to them. • Assist students with time management. • Educate and orient students to the demands of and differences in online learning. • Design high-quality courses and programs that are learner-focused and responsive to student needs.
Community building	• Make community building an instructor/facilitator priority. • Focus on keeping students engaged with the course and with one another. • Empower students to take responsibility for community building by encouraging student leadership and rotating facilitation. • Encourage high levels of interactivity by calling on silent students and contacting individual students who are not actively participating.
Group size	• If at all possible, keep group size in online courses at fifteen or fewer. • When larger courses are offered, divide the group into smaller discussion groups with rotated leadership. • Minimize the numbers involved in chat sessions and include no more than ten in synchronous work.
Faculty/Student appropriateness for online learning	• Encourage self-assessment for appropriateness for online work among both faculty and students. • Offer both online and face-to-face versions of required courses.

	• Do not force faculty or students into online courses, but encourage them to try.
Obstacles	• Ensure access to technology.
	• Design courses with accessibility in mind.
	• Design courses that fit well with the curriculum and are learner-focused.
	• Provide comprehensive student services to virtual students.
	• Address all learning styles and barriers to learning, such as disabilities, when designing courses.
	• Provide adequate training and support for students.
	• Make sure instructors have good training and develop good online facilitation skills.
	• Promote a sense of community both in the class and in the institution.
	• Be flexible when life intervenes, through the use of extensions and incomplete grades, allowing for course and assignment completion when circumstances return to normal.

CHAPTER ELEVEN

BECOMING TRULY LEARNER-FOCUSED

BEST PRACTICES IN ONLINE TEACHING

This book began with a question: What does it really mean to be learner-focused in the online environment? As we have demonstrated in our discussion of all the issues and concerns in online teaching, there are many answers to this question. The response is complex. In order to be truly learner-focused we need to:

- Understand who our students are
- Understand how they learn
- Be aware of the issues that affect their lives and learning and how they bring these issues into the classroom
- Understand what they need so we can support them in their learning
- Understand how to assist them in their development as reflective practitioners
- Find a way to involve them in course design and assessment
- Respect their rights as learners and their role in the learning process
- Understand how to develop courses and programs with an eye to continuous quality improvement so that our students stay with the learning process and can move smoothly toward their goals, objectives, and dreams

Certainly, these principles apply in face-to-face situations as well as online. But in the online environment, as we have stressed throughout the book, we need to be much more deliberate in paying attention to who our students are and what they need because we are not physically seeing or interacting with them on a daily basis.

Being Learner-Focused in the Online Environment

Maryellen Weimer (2002) notes: "Being learner-centered focuses attention squarely on learning: what the student is learning, how the student is learning, the conditions under which the student is learning, whether the student is retaining and applying the learning, and how current learning positions the student for future learning" (p. xvi). In her discussion of face-to-face teaching situations, Weimer outlines five key changes that need to occur for learner-centered teaching to take place: the balance of power needs to change, the function of content needs to change, the role of the teacher needs to change, the responsibility for learning needs to change, and the purpose and processes of evaluation need to change. Let us look at each as it applies to online learning:

The Balance of Power Needs to Change

In effective online learning, the instructor acts as a facilitator, encouraging students to take charge of their own learning process. We have often discussed the need for the instructor to move out of the middle, vacating the "sage on the stage" role and becoming the "guide on the side." Does this mean that instructors also need to vacate their role as content experts? The answer to that question is a resounding *no*. In order to guide students effectively toward the acquisition of knowledge in a given subject, instructors have to be content experts in that subject. They can then assist students in evaluating the websites they visit, the material they bring back to the group, and the material they are reading. As content experts, instructors create the container for learning, establishing meaningful boundaries to the area and helping students to stay on track. However, they are not the fount from which knowledge flows. Thus, how instructors create this container is the key.

Management of the online classroom experience is not authoritarian. In other words, if an instructor encourages students to work with one another and encourages those students who gravitate toward the process management role to exercise it, then the authority for managing the learning experience will be shared. Thus, a learner-centered online experience becomes a more shared, more democratic classroom experience.

The Function of Content Needs to Change

Carr-Chellman and Ducastel (2001) note that a good online course design makes learning resources and instructional activities available to students instead of providing instruction. The difference between the two is allowing students the opportunity to work together to create knowledge and meaning, rather than providing facts and information that they memorize and retain in some fashion. The former provides the opportunity for the development of critical thinking skills, whereas the latter may not.

Once again, when we talk about content, the issue of teaching in different disciplines emerges. Is it really possible to co-create knowledge and meaning when the content area is mathematics, for example? We recently met an instructor who would say yes, it is possible to co-create knowledge and meaning in a mathematics class. Besides providing basic material that students have to memorize and retain, he incorporates "problem groups" into his online mathematics courses. He divides the class into collaborative small groups and provides a series of problems for each one to try to solve together. Each problem has a different time line attached to it, depending on the complexity of the work involved. Together, the students seek out the content that will allow them to find the solution to the problem and explain how they got to that solution. Their solutions and explanations are then shared with the larger group. Thus, the process of learning collaboratively becomes the focus, not the content itself. This instructor is convinced that his students learn and retain as much or more information about mathematics than they would if he used a "memorize-and-retain" approach alone.

The Role of the Teacher Needs to Change

Weimer (2002) notes that in the learner-centered environment, the instructor is no longer the *key* content expert. As we noted earlier, the instructor in an online class moves to the side and allows student expertise to emerge. Weimer states, "If the goal of teaching is to promote learning, then the role the teacher takes to accomplish that goal changes considerably" (p. 14).

This does not mean that the instructor does not have a role to play in the delivery of a learner-centered online course. In a review of student attitudes toward online teaching and learning, Goldsmith (2001) reported that students appreciate having a knowledgeable faculty member who is actively involved in the course. Learner-centered online instructors have a significant contribution to make to the learning experience, and students want to know they are present and involved. Sometimes the instructor role involves acting as another student in the group—this occurs, for example when facilitation is rotated among all of the students in the group—and sometimes the instructor is the main facilitator. The key is to be flexible and willing to do what the group needs for the learning process. In this way, the students and their learning remain the focus of attention.

The Responsibility for Learning Needs to Change

Clearly, if the instructor acts as a guide and facilitator, then the students need to take responsibility for their own learning process. As we have said many times, students get out of an online course what they put into it, and this is a message that they need to hear from the beginning of the course to its conclusion. They need to be encouraged and empowered to take charge of the formation of the learning community, to interact with one another—not just the instructor—and to receive feedback on how well (or not) this is occurring. The tag line we like to use to close our faculty development sessions is "We are all the experts when it comes to our own learning." We believe that this statement conveys a couple of things: first, that we have as much to learn from our students as they do from us—we are not the sole experts in the learning process—and second, that students need to take responsibility for the process and teach one another. The following post from Nita, a graduate student new to online learning, illustrates this point:

As a virtual student and having had the opportunity to participate in the virtual learning environment, I can without reservation say that I am indeed processing and earning a reality based degree. An initial perception in the academic world indicates that on-line or virtual degrees are not really degrees because of the lack of face-to-face communication and the social affiliation attributed to the classroom environment. This proves to be false as virtual students develop strengths and expertise from their experience and exposure to the virtual classroom and the participants it contains, most directly through the leadership of an effective virtual facilitator. The keyboard and the internet become the tools for effective communication and learning, and complete validation that the human mind is the reality based driver for this virtual educational experience. *Nita*

The Purpose and Processes of Evaluation Need to Change

What do students learn in an online course? Is that learning less than or equal to the learning in face-to-face situations? How do we know? How do we measure outcomes? These are all questions that are frequently raised with regard to online learning, based on a sense that because there is no face-to-face contact in a course delivered completely online, it is somehow a lesser experience. As we discussed in Chapter Eight, evaluation that is in alignment with learning objectives for the course and is consistent with the types of learning activities embedded in the course is likely to yield information about outcomes that is useful not only from the standpoint of course improvement but also from the standpoint of student learning. Including self-assessment in that process encourages students to reflect on their learning and demonstrate their mastery of course concepts. The following student reflection is not only a reflection on learning but on the achievement of learning goals in an online class:

I must say this was truly a growth class for me. I have studied change before and was thrown a bit when I first started this class in trying to see how things linked together, from Animal Dreams to globalization. The readings and interactions created intense reflection and a new paradigm for me in looking at change beyond the mechanics of it.

I enjoyed responding and reading responses to the postings. The timelines and amount needed on the responses allowed a convenient yet thorough discussion to take place. The many learners in the class created a wealth of insight to the readings. I was able to fully express my views to each response and received much feedback that I felt validated my thoughts. Many of these thoughts were from my new paradigm versus my old positions. They allowed me to carry them into work and practice.

In each posting I responded in the same manner as those other learners I appreciated. I wrote to validate their thoughts, express what parts I learned from them, and I inquired for better understanding or more information as needed to either comprehend their thoughts more fully or gain more knowledge about a concept they introduced.

Since this was one of my first two net classes, I was pleased with the format. I took full advantage of it and was serious in compliance to the rubric both in my sharing responses to the postings and to other learners. I appreciate your feedback and the several learners that I learned to respect and learn from their sharing. Even though some other students may not have given input that I felt moved by or significant, I can say that I gained something from each of them in some positive way. *Glenn*

O'Reilly and Newton (2001) indicate that students value online discussions, whether or not those discussions figure into the evaluation scheme for the course. This student's reflections illustrate the benefit he gained from interacting with others online, both in terms of his own learning and his perceived contribution to the learning of his colleagues.

Traditional means of evaluation, such as exams and quizzes, do not really assess the contribution that online discussion makes to learning. Consequently, as we consider how to evaluate outcomes from online courses, as well as the courses themselves, we need to abandon comparisons with face-to-face learning and develop means by which the benefits of online learning can be assessed on their own.

A part of doing that, if we take a learner-focused position, is to look at the impact of online learning on the learner and assess what we need to do at each of our institutions and in each of our courses to address all learners' needs. The field of online teaching also needs to more thoroughly research those impacts in order to more effectively address best practices. We can then begin to modify our courses and programs to reflect the information we gather.

What the Online Learner Wants

At the start of this book, we noted that satisfaction levels for online learners tend to be low. Hara and Kling (2000) attribute this to the fact that online learners experience points of distress in an online course related to the technology in use, particularly when there is a lack of technical support, and in the areas of course content and communication. They note that the literature on online learning is replete with tips for instructors and administrators, but it rarely addresses students and their needs online. They attribute most of the distress of online learners to the fact that courses are developed and taught by instructors with little or no training in online instruction. They note that higher-quality courses tend to be taught by experienced, dedicated instructors who understand the experience of the virtual student. According to Hara and Kling, students said they needed the following in an online course:

- Reassurance that the ideas they are posting to an online discussion are on track
- Clear instructions about course expectations and for completing assignments
- The ability to express dissatisfaction with the level and quality of instructor communication in the course and with the course itself without fear of repercussion
- A reasonable load in terms of the amount of reading, postings, and e-mails required
- Prompt, unambiguous feedback
- An orientation to the technology in use
- Technical support

Hara and Kling (2000) conclude by calling for additional student-centered studies of online learning "that are designed to teach us how the appropriate use of technology and pedagogy could make distance education more beneficial for more students. In addition, we need ways to translate the best of such research into the practitioner literature" (Understanding Instructional Work and Communication in Practice, ¶ 4). Our teaching practice online needs to be more learner-centered, but so does our research that informs such practice.

In sum, what the virtual student wants and needs is very clear: communication and feedback, interactivity and a sense of community, and adequate direction and

empowerment to carry out the tasks required for the course. If we attempt to repli-
cate the face-to-face classroom in the online environment, we will not meet these
needs and instead cause the frustration and distress that Hara and Kling describe.
The solution is to focus on best practices that are learner-centered and that strive
to meet the needs and wants of the virtual student.

A Focus on Best Practices

Although there is an ever-expanding body of literature on best practices in online
teaching, we find that it is frequently limited to the inclusion of certain types of
technical tools in an online course and rarely focuses on learner-centered pedagogical practices. For example, a best practice described might be to increase
communication by making greater use of the discussion board. Although the discussion board is a sound means for communicating online, how often should an
instructor post to the board? How rapidly should an instructor respond to student
questions and concerns? Simply using the board is not a best practice; it is just a
vehicle for getting there.

Graham, Kursat, Byung-Ro, Craner, and Duffy (2001) chose to apply Chickering and Gamson's "Seven Principles of Good Practice in Undergraduate Education," a well-used framework for evaluating good teaching that was originally
published in 1987, as a means of developing a list of best practices in online education. For each of the seven principles, the authors provided a corresponding
lesson for online learning, which comes much closer to a working best practices
list for online instruction. We add to their discussion based on the principles we
have been discussing in this book.

Principle 1: Good Practice Encourages Student-Faculty Contact

Lesson for online instruction: Instructors should provide clear guidelines for interaction with students.

Graham and colleagues are suggesting here that instructors delineate categories of communication and inform students about which messages to send to
the instructor and which to send elsewhere, such as to technical support personnel. Although this is important, we do not feel it is critical to the successful delivery of an online course. They also suggest, however, that instructors set clear
standards for response times to student messages. This is a far more critical factor
in making students feel supported by the instructor. Establishing a reasonable turn-
around time—such as twenty-four or forty-eight hours to respond to student
e-mail or three to five days to respond to an assignment—and then making every

effort to live up to that schedule will help students feel reassured that they are on the right track, and that the instructor is paying attention. This is a critical component of student satisfaction with online learning.

Principle 2: Good Practice Encourages Cooperation Among Students

Lesson for online instruction: Well-designed discussion assignments facilitate meaningful cooperation among students.

As we have noted, the ability to engage in collaborative work is a hallmark of online learning and the foundation of a learning community. Going beyond online discussion to include small group work and other means by which students can collaborate helps to broaden and deepen the learning, lessens the sense of isolation that many online students feel, and allows students to test out ideas and feel a sense of connection to the course, the instructor, and the group. In general, higher levels of satisfaction with online learning occur when collaboration is an integral part of the course design.

Principle 3: Good Practice Encourages Active Learning

Lesson for online instruction: Students should present course projects.

Although presenting projects and papers online and receiving feedback on work are critical collaborative means of extending the learning process, the possibilities for active learning in the online classroom go far beyond this. Asking students to engage with real-life examples and problems, participate in simulations, or go out into their communities to research an issue and report back to the group are a few of the kinds of active learning techniques that can be incorporated into an online class. Creative course design means doing more than reading and discussing. When active learning techniques are included, they help to engage the virtual student in the learning process.

Principle 4: Good Practice Gives Prompt Feedback

Lesson for online instruction: Instructors need to provide two types of feedback: information feedback and acknowledgment feedback.

Instructors need to find a balance in the amount and frequency of their online feedback so that students know that they are present and paying attention, but not so much that they overwhelm the group or dominate the discussion. The instructor-facilitator role in the online discussion is to assist students in synthesizing material, seeing parallels, and helping to summarize major points, thus helping them move forward. Too much instructor intervention will effectively stop all conversation as the instructor takes center stage. But not enough instructor intervention will also stop conversation because students may become confused and unsure about what is expected. Achieving a good balance, therefore, is the key.

Principle 5: Good Practice Emphasizes Time on Task

Lesson for online instruction: Online courses need deadlines.

Graham and colleagues state: "Regularly distributed deadlines encourage students to spend time on tasks and help students with busy schedules avoid procrastination. They also provide a context for regular contact with the instructor and peers" (Good Practice Emphasizes Time on Task, ¶ 1).Because virtual students need to manage time effectively in order to complete an online course successfully, providing structure in the form of posting and assignment deadlines helps them to get through the course without getting stalled or lost along the way. Deadlines also provide benchmarks for evaluating progress. Too often, online students come to the end of a course with little idea of how they are being evaluated. Assignments with deadlines for completion and regular feedback from the instructor and other student colleagues help to provide a road map for the virtual student and assist with successful course completion.

Principle 6: Good Practice Communicates High Expectations

Lesson for online instruction: Challenging tasks, sample cases, and praise for quality work communicate high expectations.

The main criticism lobbed at online instruction is that it is not as rigorous as its face-to-face counterpart. By creating assignments and tasks that are challenging and holding students to high standards of assignment completion, we can create online courses that surpass the face-to-face experience. "Dumbing down" the curriculum for online delivery should not be an option. Some believe that because content is delivered differently online, that means it is being simplified. However, if we challenge students to explore the territory of the course thoroughly and demand active participation in that process, the result should be deep learning and high quality results.

Principle 7: Good Practice Respects Diverse Talents and Ways of Learning

Lesson for online instruction: Allowing students to choose project topics allows diverse views to emerge.

Besides the area of topic selection, online learning can and should be responsive to all learning styles and cultural, ethnic, gender, and geographic differences—

it should find ways for all voices to be heard. Collaborative learning activities allow students to work from their strengths while exploring the material for the course. If the types of activities in an online course are varied, students can employ their preferred learning styles while also developing less preferred styles. Overall, instructors need to seek out and include means by which various opinions and ways of life are honored in the learning process.

Concluding Thoughts

Table 11.1 summarizes our thoughts on best practices for learner-focused online teaching. We close the book with this table, as a way of bringing together the ideas we have been sharing throughout, and also in an attempt to make a contribution to the paucity of available literature on best practices online.

As the field of online distance learning evolves, so will our thoughts about what constitutes best practice. However, by focusing on inclusion, collaboration, flexibility, good communication, and interaction—no matter what discipline is being taught—an online instructor cannot go wrong, and the virtual student is sure to benefit from the experience. This is what it means to be truly learner-centered.

What follows this last chapter are the two resources in our Toolkit for a Successful Online Student. We hope that if these tools are used in more online courses, they will help more virtual students have a quality experience, develop critical thinking and reflection skills, and become empowered, lifelong learners. A review of the tools should also offer ideas and alternatives to instructors in the course design process and answer questions about how to do such things as develop a good, comprehensive set of guidelines for an online course. We ask our readers to use the tools as you see fit—our goal is to make online learning the best possible experience it can be for all virtual students.

TABLE 11.1. BEST PRACTICES IN ONLINE TEACHING.

Virtual Student Focus	Institutional and Instructor Best Practices
Understanding who our students are	• Begin the course by having students post introductions and share learning objectives so as to get to know our students as people. • Create a social space in the course so that students can relax with one another and the instructor. • Humanize the course site by making it warm and inviting. • Use humor appropriately to engage students in the discussion and encourage them to do the same.

TABLE 11.1.   (*CONTINUED*).

Virtual Student Focus	Institutional and Instructor Best Practices
Understanding how our students learn	• Become knowledgeable about the issues involved in working with different learning styles. • Respect different learning styles and encourage students to respect one another by posting appropriate feedback and working with each other's strengths. • Design courses with varied activities in order to tap into various learning styles. • Provide assignment choices so that students can tap into their strengths.
Awareness of the issues that affect students' lives and learning and how they bring them into the classroom	• Encourage students to contact the instructor and the group if life intervenes and interferes with their participation in the course and reach out to them if they do not. • Encourage students to bring real-life examples into the classroom to illustrate concepts being discussed or to apply those concepts to their lives. • Be aware of the impact of isolation and the other factors that can influence a student's participation in a course, and be flexible in working with students to resolve or work around those issues.
Understanding what virtual students need to support them in their learning.	• The institution should develop and provide comprehensive student services programs to serve virtual students. • The institution should designate support personnel to assist virtual students. • Round-the-clock technical support should be provided to students. • Students should receive technical training so that they can access their courses easily. • The students' technical skills should be evaluated, and the institution or instructor should suggest ways of improving those skills to eliminate potential problems with online courses.
Understanding how to assist virtual students in their development as reflective practitioners	• Develop collaborative course activities that promote reflection. • Provide guidelines for students in developing critical thinking skills. • Provide guidelines for students to assist them in giving and receiving good feedback. • Ask students to reflect on their overall learning in the course at least once midway and again at the end of the course.
Finding a means to involve virtual students in course design and assessment	• At the beginning of the course, ask students to post their learning objectives and how they feel they will meet them through the course.

- Ask students regularly for feedback on how the course is going for them and for any suggestions for improvement.
- Be responsive to student suggestions for improvement and flexible enough to incorporate those that make sense while the course is in progress.
- Incorporate course evaluations that go beyond instructor popularity polls, such as letters to successors, and give students points or credit for their contributions.

Respecting students' rights as learners and their role in the learning process

- Both the institution and the instructor should respect student privacy by not sharing their work or contributions to a course without getting their consent or inviting anyone to view the course without their permission.
- Provide prompt, honest, and respectful feedback to students on their work and in response to their e-mails—establish and adhere to guidelines for response time and make students aware of those time lines.
- View student contributions to an online course as their intellectual property and treat them as such.
- Empower students to take charge of the learning process and work with one another to form a strong learning community by establishing participation guidelines on talking directly to one another without an instructor there as a filter.

Understanding how to develop courses and programs with an eye to continuous quality improvement so that students stay in the learning process and move smoothly in the direction of their goals, objectives, and dreams

- Develop courses that are specifically designed for online learning and not a replica of the face-to-face classroom; they should be rigorous and contain clear expectations for course completion, clear directions for assignments and participation, and a reasonable workload.
- Be creative in assignment development, allowing for student choice in assignment completion and promoting collaboration and reflection.
- Reach out to students who are not participating at required levels to determine why and to bring them back into the course.
- Develop courses that contain relevant content, are interactive, and are cohesive with the other courses in a student's program of study.
- Most importantly, remember that there are people at the other end of the wire who need their instructors to be open, honest, responsive, flexible, respectful, empowering, and most of all, present in the learning experience.

~

RESOURCES: THE TOOLKIT FOR A SUCCESSFUL ONLINE STUDENT

INTRODUCTION TO THE TOOLKIT
FOR A SUCCESSFUL ONLINE STUDENT

A s we have presented our numerous faculty workshops across the United States, Canada, and Europe, we have been asked repeatedly to share the materials we have gathered over our years of teaching online that we have found to be particularly useful in course design and delivery. This Toolkit for a Successful Online Student is a collection of those materials. It is meant to be a stand-alone piece for faculty and students to use to assist with successful completion of online courses. Some of the tools are original works of our own design, and others are adaptations of material from our colleagues. We have given credit to those who have contributed to our learning and are grateful to them for the work they are doing in service of students.

The toolkit is divided into two sections: Resource A contains faculty tools and Resource B contains student tools. All of the tools may be incorporated into a syllabus or as part of an online course. We have organized them in this way simply to provide ease of use and to indicate the primary user of each. The faculty tools section contains the following:

- *Sample course guidelines,* including content and posting guidelines, participation guidelines, course teaching and learning methods, and various means of communicating faculty and student expectations
- A guide to developing critical thinking skills
- A guide to developing good discussion questions for the online course

- A guide to using case study methodology
- A guide to evaluating student work, including another sample grading rubric for an online course

The student section contains these tools:

- Self-assessment for online learning
- Tips for being a successful online learner
- Communication tools, including emoticons, acronyms, and netiquette (These elements could easily have been included in the faculty tools but we chose to place them in this section to provide communication guidance to virtual students.)
- Guidelines for giving feedback
- Time management tools
- Tips for writing research and reflection papers

Numerous websites exist on the Internet to support faculty and student work in online courses and can be additional sources of material. Some of the more useful sites are these:

MERLOT (Multimedia Educational Resource for Learning and Online Teaching) is a free membership site with links to online learning materials along with annotations and peer reviews. This is a great site for getting ideas and sharing experiences of online teaching and learning [*www.merlot.org*].

The *World Lecture Hall* is another site that maintains free materials contributed by faculty giving courses online or in blended format [*www.utexas.edu/world/lecture/*].

The *Western Cooperative for Educational Telecommunications,* found on the WICHE (Western Interstate Commission for Higher Education) site, offers a guide to the development of good online student services programs [*www.wiche.edu/Telecom/resources/publications/guide/guide.htm*].

StudentAffairs.com is a comprehensive and useful site for student affairs professionals that offers everything from job listings to listservs and links to other resources [*www.StudentAffairs.com*]. The website also contains an area entitled "Student Pulse Online," where links to websites designed mainly by students can be found along with evaluations of those sites [*http://www.studentaffairs.com/web/pulse.html*].

The *ERIC/CASS* system contains a wealth of resources and cyberlibraries containing information on issues affecting students, such as substance abuse and violence, and also contains full-text articles about such issues as cyber-counseling [*http://ericcass.uncg.edu/*].

The *University of Chicago Student Counseling and Resource Service* provides a collection of pamphlets and books related to various student services issues, including study skills, writing, time management, and family issues [*http://counseling.uchicago.edu/vpc/virtulets.html*].

The following are websites where comparisons of the various course management software, or courseware, can be found. The comparisons can be particularly useful to faculty unfamiliar with the courseware packages commonly used and for those in the process of choosing courseware:

- *Edutools* is a site that was built to assist educators in decision making by reviewing the many options for course management systems [*http://www.c2t2.ca/landonline/techinfo.html#tabletop*].
- "Criteria for Evaluating Courseware Applications" is an article that provides criteria to help readers decide which software to choose [*http://rilw.emp.paed.uni-muenchen.de/99/papers/Perniu.html*].
- The *Maricopa Center for Learning and Instruction* has created a website that houses links to a number of reviews of courseware [*http://www.mcli.dist.maricopa.edu/ocotillo/courseware/compare.html*].

RESOURCE A

FACULTY TOOLS

Sample Course Guidelines

The following guidelines cover a number of issues in an online course. The first set covers content and posting, the second participation, the next set course teaching and learning methods, and the last set presents various means of communicating faculty and student expectations. These guidelines can be used separately or in combination, creating a comprehensive set of guidelines for a course. We generally use parts or all of these guidelines in our syllabi and modify them based on the educational level of the student (community college, undergraduate, graduate, or continuing education) and the degree of structure we feel the group needs. Because we have used numerous courseware applications in the delivery of our courses, the guidelines may refer to a particular feature in a courseware package. Instructors who choose to adopt these guidelines will need to adapt them to the courseware in use at their institutions.

Content and Posting Guidelines

Here is some additional information and suggestions to assist you with this course:

1. The most predictable breakdown occurs whenever participants are late in posting their papers and responses. This is often the result of business trips,

illnesses, overload, and computer glitches—but be aware that the responses and learning of your peers depend upon your timely contributions. Call me as soon as possible if a situation arises that will affect a due date or your peers, and post a message to the group. Switch dates with a colleague if needed. Remember to post messages regularly, even just to say you're still out there—your colleagues will greatly appreciate it.

2. I will be constructing the course site with a folder for assignments. I will post the assignments as major topic areas within the folder. Please post your papers as the next level of response to the assignments (reply to the topic). That way responses to the papers become the third level (replies to the papers), and so on. Please don't add folders to the course site, but feel free to add topics within the folders.

3. Please review the descriptions of the assignments while you work on them and before you post your assignment. A common mistake is to become intrigued with a wonderfully intriguing idea—and not address the assignment requirements.

4. You will find on the course site a folder that contains topics not directly related to the course material labeled "Group Process." One of the group topics contained is called "The Sandbox," which may be used for ongoing discussion, comments, and general relationship maintenance that do not directly relate to posting or responding to a paper. This is your "student lounge," if you will, and although I will be available and observing this process, I will generally not get too involved. The other topic in this folder is "Electronic Reflections." Feel free to use this area to comment on what it's like to learn electronically, if you want to.

5. Post replies/topics that you want me to see/respond to with "Rena" in the subject line so I can find them more easily. It will also help for searching and attention purposes if you include the name of the person in the subject line to whom you are replying—for example: Student's reply to Rena, Re: Subject.

6. Norms to ponder: Timeliness. Confidentiality within group (no sidebars, organizational and personal information is sensitive). Civility and supportive criticism. No sidebars—this means no private e-mail or conversations that discuss other members of the group. Group issues need to be dealt with in the group.

7. Using the Search Button at the discussion level may be helpful and will identify by topic/name new postings that you haven't read. You can also search the last twenty-four hours and do advanced searches here. Toggling between the table view and the dialogue view at the bottom of the originating topic may also be helpful. The table view lists all of the replies by title/name and can greatly reduce the load time and let you pick and choose replies you want to read. The dialogue view displays the entire text of all the replies and is help-

ful in maintaining continuity and context if you get lost in the who-replied-to-whom maze.

Guidelines for Online Participation

Should you have questions or comments on any of these guidelines, let's discuss them! Also, please add any guidelines that you feel are appropriate.

1. Attendance and presence are required for this class. You are expected to log on a minimum of twice per week (at any time during the week) and are expected to post a substantive contribution to the discussion at that time. Simply saying "hello" or "I agree" is not considered a substantive contribution. You must support your position or begin a new topic or add somehow to the discussion when logging on.

2. Assignments will be posted online. You will be asked to comment on and provide feedback to one another on your work.

3. Although we strongly suggest that all issues, questions, and problems be dealt with online, you can feel free to call or e-mail either of us regarding these issues at any time.

4. Use good "netiquette," such as:

   a. Check the discussion frequently and respond appropriately and on subject.

   b. Focus on one subject per message and use pertinent subject titles.

   c. Capitalize words only to highlight a point or for titles—capitalizing otherwise is generally viewed as SHOUTING!

   d. Be professional and careful with your online interaction.

   e. Cite all quotes, references, and sources.

   f. When posting a long message, it is generally considered courteous to warn readers at the beginning of the message that it is a lengthy post.

   g. It is considered extremely rude to forward someone else's messages without their permission, so always ask first.

   h. It is fine to use humor, but use it carefully. The absence of face-to-face cues can cause humor to be misinterpreted as criticism or flaming (angry, antagonistic criticism). Feel free to use emoticons such as :) or ;) to let others know that you're being humorous.

Most of all, let's have fun together! This is an exciting and relevant topic for us all. We hope that we will be able to share our thoughts and experiences with one another in the form of an active and stimulating discussion!

Note: These "netiquette" guidelines were adapted from Arlene H. Rinaldi's article "The Net User Guidelines and Netiquette" (http://www.fau.edu/netiquette/net/).

Course Schedule. Discussion questions for the week will be posted on Monday evenings so that we can begin discussion of the topic by Wednesday of each week. Kicking off a discussion means posting some of your reflections and thoughts about the readings and/or posts from the previous week that lead into the current week's topics. If you cite the readings or another post, please include your references and page numbers so that we can all follow your thinking. Your post should be no longer than a page. First responses to the ideas, questions, or readings will be due by Wednesday of each week. We will post discussion questions for your consideration weekly. Consider the questions in relationship to the readings and post a one-page narrative representing your views and reflections.

Case studies will also be due on Monday by twelve midnight Pacific time.

Overall participation will be worth twenty points.

Course Teaching and Learning Methods. (*Note*: The following was developed for a hybrid or web-enhanced course in which students met face-to-face and then continued their work together on a discussion board.)

Because this course is being taught in intensive format, it is very important for students to keep up with reading assignments and online discussions of the reading. Questions will be posted by the instructor on the course site on a weekly basis to stimulate the discussion. Responses do not need to be addressed to the instructor but can and should be in response to the thoughts and ideas of other students as well. When posting to the online discussion, please keep good netiquette in mind. Do not use all capital letters or others will think you are SHOUTING. Do keep your responses professional and respectful. Using "emoticons" such as :) or ;) to indicate that you are joking or teasing is appropriate. If something angers you, do not respond immediately. Wait and carefully formulate your response so that it is respectful. We hope to engage in lively discussion online!

During the intensives (face-to-face sessions), instruction will consist of minimal lecture, a great deal of discussion, small group work generally around a case study or simulation, some use of video, and presentations by students. I see my role as your instructor as a "learning facilitator" and not a lecturer. I hope that you will take a great deal of responsibility for your own learning.

Faculty and Student Expectations

The following paragraphs contain our suggestions for how to present faculty and student expectations. The first sections contain information that we include in a course syllabus; the later sections take the form of a welcome letter to students that we post on the discussion board of an online course.

Student Responsibilities

1. Students will do the required readings for each class according to the class schedule, and will actively participate in online discussions. Students will make a minimum of two original posts and two responses to other students' posts during a week. The quality of comments is more important than the quantity, so students are expected to be reflective in their posts and responses.
2. Students will identify ways in which their learning goals and objectives fit with the class readings and will post a reflection on their learning objectives during the first week of class.
3. In the first week of the class, students will send an e-mail to the instructor to present ideas for their final class project. All projects must be approved by the instructor.
4. Students will design and complete a final project for the course. Students are encouraged to review the relevant literature in their research area to frame the project and are expected to read and reference at least three sources beyond the required reading for the class. The nature, writing style, and length of the report will depend on the particular approach students select for their research. However, APA format is expected.
5. Students will also write a two- to three-page critical reflection paper on their learning in this course. More guidance on the completion of the two required papers can be found elsewhere in the syllabus.
6. Students will participate in a small group collaborative case study analysis that will involve critical interpretation of a particular issue related to the course. Small groups will be assigned by the instructor during the second week of class. Groups will be expected to work together from Week 5 to 8 on their collaborative assignment.
7. Students will either watch a film or read a novel selected from the list collaboratively put together by the students and instructor during the first week of the class related to the course content. They will then write a critical review (five to seven pages minimum) that will be posted on the course website. Students are expected to comment on at least two reviews submitted by their peers.
8. Students will make a final online presentation of the key findings from their final project during the last week of class.
9. Students will follow the APA guidelines for all written assignments.
10. Students will write a self-evaluation of learning, which will be due the last class.

Instructor Responsibilities

1. Instructor will engage students in a discussion by bringing out the key issues from the assigned readings and raising relevant questions.
2. Instructor will provide reactions to student responses and discussion in order to clarify certain ideas and concepts being discussed.
3. Instructor will provide opportunities for group work in class that will include discussion as well as hands-on exercises.
4. Instructor will arrange for guest speakers to visit and participate in an online synchronous chat with students, as appropriate.
5. Instructor will provide updated information on relevant resources for various topics of interest.
6. Instructor will read and critically assess students' assignments, and provide timely feedback.
7. Instructor will respond to all student e-mails within forty-eight hours of receipt.
8. Instructor will evaluate student progress in the class and write a midterm and final narrative evaluation for each student.

Sample Expectations Letter

Dear Learners,

We co-teach in a way that is probably unfamiliar to most of you. So we will attempt to clarify our roles in the hope that you will understand why we do what we do and why we are successful at our endeavors.

We have been working together for over ten years now as students, researchers, well-known writers, professors, and not least of all, friends. Having said this let us assure you that we still learn from our students and that is the reason for this message.

When we conduct a learning experience, build a community, facilitate a session or guide a group of students we use methods that have proven in research, theory, and practice to work for us. In this class, you will note that we will respond to issues, concerns and questions in one voice. These means that when there is a response posted in the class it is posted after we have had a discussion, have debated and discussed the issue or concern, and are in agreement as to what should be posted.

In some classes Dr. Palloff posts these responses; in some classes Dr. Pratt posts them. We have been working this way for years and have found it to be effective in many ways and probably the most effective in all cases.

We realize that this has caused some concern in some classes, but let us assure you in advance that we will discuss between us virtually every issue and question that will be posted in this class, meaning that we will both have read them and have decided which way to approach whatever the issue or concern is.

We hope this has clarified our roles as professors and mentors. Should you have questions about any of this, or anything else for that matter, please don't hesitate to contact us. We're here to facilitate your learning experience!

Please respond to us either by e-mail or by responding to this post that you have read and understood this announcement. Should you have questions about this, please ask!

We look forward to working with all of you, and again, offer our sincere welcome! Hugs to all,
Keith and Rena

To all SC501 learners:

Welcome to the class! The following are some guidelines that will help you successfully navigate and complete this class. Please read them and the syllabus and then post a message in response to this one telling me that you've read, understand, and agree with the guidelines:

1. If you have never taken a previous online class, please go into the syllabus (found under the "Schedule" icon on this course site) and do the sample class/tour of Learning Space. The syllabus states: "If this is your first online class, start here." Follow the directions and take the tour! It will help you immensely—I promise!

2. DO NOT, UNDER ANY CIRCUMSTANCES, USE THE "FACULTY START NEW TOPIC" BUTTON IN THE COURSE ROOM!!! If it seems like I'm shouting this at you, you're right, I am! :) This button has very limited function in an online course in Learning Space and can only serve to mess up people's ability to track the discussion. I use the button to start the week's discussion, and I am the only one who should be using it. All of your responses MUST be posted by using the "COMMENT" Button. To post to the discussion, click on the subject line of the post, read the post (be it my questions or someone's response to my question), and then comment by using the Comment Button. What happens as the result of using the wrong button to start topics is what I call "jungle syndrome." The discussion becomes chaotic and hard to follow. So please, please, please, follow these directions.

3. Questions about using Learning Space, about books, or about issues unrelated to the course content should be either posted in The Café or e-mailed to me. I will be posting a Café every week, so DO NOT START A NEW TOPIC TO ASK THESE QUESTIONS!

4. I post the discussion questions for the week on Sunday evening or Monday morning. I expect your first response to the questions by Wednesday and second response toward the end of the week. DO NOT POST ALL OF YOUR RESPONSES ON THE SAME DAY! We are attempting to build a learning community here, and therefore, depend on everyone's participation. If it all happens on weekends, those people who are looking for input into the discussion during the week are left hanging. Try to log in a few times each week and definitely post on different days.

5. The reading for this course includes three small books that are available through the bookstore and a course pack available through XanEdu. Directions for accessing your materials through XanEdu are in the Media Center.

6. And speaking of the Media Center, you'll find that there are Media Center assignments in some units of the course. What that means is that the reading is

located in the Media Center. The discussion related to that reading, however, will happen here in the Course Room.

7. You'll find a grading rubric in the Media Center for use with your discussion postings and research paper. Please review it and ask questions if you have any.

OK, that's all the hollering I plan to do! :) I really do hope that you enjoy your experience in this class. I'm here to facilitate your learning and support you through this process. I sincerely welcome you to Capella and to SC501 and look forward to working with all of you.

As previously stated, I'd like everyone to post a reply to this message indicating that you've read and understand it. If you don't understand something, please ask questions by using the Comment Button and I will respond here. I want everyone to be able to learn from each other's questions.

Thanks, everyone, and let's have fun out there!

Rena

Guidelines for Developing Critical Thinking Skills

Critical thinking skills can be developed. The following guidelines are divided into two sections—the first offers some ideas for students to allow them to begin thinking about critical thinking and what it entails. The second contains some tips for promoting the development of critical thinking in an online course.

Thinking About Critical Thinking

In order to become critical thinkers there are several things we must do:

- *Clarity:* We must be clear about our ideas and how they are expressed.
- *Consistency:* We must be consistent in our behavior and thinking.
- *Openness:* We must open ourselves to the process of learning and seek learning anytime and anywhere.
- *Evaluation:* We must be willing to go beyond what is on the surface and evaluate material, analyze it, and synthesize it, using our life experiences as a guide.
- *Communication:* We must have the ability to communicate our thoughts so that others can understand our thinking.
- *Specificity:* We must be specific and focused in our feedback and communications.
- *Accessibility:* We must be perceived as being accessible and willing to discuss our thoughts, even if they are unpopular or different from those of others.
- *Flexibility:* We must be open to new ideas and new ways of doing business.
- *Courage to take risks:* We must have the courage to take the risk to express our

own opinions and offer feedback to others, even if our opinions do not "go with the flow."

Tips for Promoting Critical Thinking Skills in an Online Class

- Encourage students to find analogies and other kinds of relationships between pieces of information in course readings and discussions.
- Provide problems or cases that students can work with and encourage them to find and evaluate alternative solutions to those problems or cases.
- Promote interactivity—discussion helps students to look at issues from a number of viewpoints.
- Discourage "groupthink." When students begin to create a chorus of "I agree's," jump into the discussion and challenge the assumptions or ask students to look at the issue in another way.
- Ask students to justify and explain their positions. Push students to provide substantive postings in response to discussion questions.
- Ask open-ended questions that promote thinking and analysis. Do not ask for lists or yes/no questions. If a yes/no question needs to be asked, require a justification for the position taken.
- Use the asynchronous nature of the online environment to promote reflection and analysis. Ask a difficult question and then tell students that you do not want an answer for two or three days to allow them to think and formulate a response.
- Ask students to apply their learning to real-life situations and to discuss how they have done that. Ask them to find examples in real life that illustrate the concepts being discussed.
- Encourage the potential spirit of discovery in an online class. Ask students to seek out and share material with one another.

Guide to Developing Good Discussion Questions for the Online Course

In their book *Discussion as a Way of Teaching*, Brookfield and Preskill (1999) offer several categories of questions to stimulate and maintain discussion. The following is a summary and digest of those categories and questions to assist instructors in creating discussion questions for an online course. (See Brookfield and Preskill, 1999, pp. 87–91, for the full text of the questions.) Another good resource in the development of questions for online courses is the article "A Framework for Designing Questions for Online Learning," by Lin Muilenburg and Zane Berge (2000).

Questions That Ask for More Evidence

- How do you know that?
- What data is that claim based on?
- What do others say that support your argument?
- Where did you find that view expressed in the materials?
- What evidence would you give to someone who doubted your interpretation?

Questions That Ask for Clarification

- Can you put that another way?
- What's a good example of what you are talking about?
- What do you mean by that?
- Can you explain the term you just used?
- Could you give a different illustration of your point?

Open-Ended Questions

- Sauvage says that when facing moral crises, people who agonize don't act, and people who act don't agonize. What does this mean? (Follow-up question: Can you think of an example that is consistent with Sauvage's maxim and another that conflicts with it?)
- Racism pervaded American society throughout the twentieth century. What are some signs that racial discrimination still exists in hiring? What are other signs that racism has abated significantly?
- Why do you think many people devote their lives to education despite the often low pay and poor working conditions?

Linking or Extension Questions

- Is there any connection between what you've just said and what Rajiv was saying a moment ago?
- How does your comment fit in with Neng's earlier comment?
- How does your observation relate to what the group decided last week?
- Does your idea challenge or support what we seem to be saying?
- How does that contribution add to what has already been said?

Hypothetical Questions

- If you were presented with the following question in an interview, how would you respond: Was your previous job full of purposeful play or drudgery and work?
- You only have two years to live and will do so with your usual energy and vitality. What will you do with your last two years?

- You just won a $100 million lottery jackpot. What will you do with the rest of your life?

Cause-and-Effect Questions

- What is likely to be the effect of changing from a one-on-one mode of working to a group mode?
- How might delivering our courses using the Internet affect our students' learning process?

Summary-and-Synthesis Questions

- What are the one or two most important ideas that emerged from this discussion?
- What remains unresolved or contentious about this topic?
- What do you understand better as a result of today's discussion?
- Based on our discussion today, what do we need to talk about next time if we're to understand this issue better?

Case Methodology: How to Analyze Cases

Note: In our seminars for faculty, we often discuss the use of case studies as a collaborative learning tool. As a result, we have been asked to include material on the case study method to assist faculty in developing collaborative assignments using this kind of material.

Using Case Studies

You are likely to find case studies used to some degree in your courses. Cases may take a variety of forms, but they are usually narratives of situations that you will be asked to explore critically. You may also be asked to find and present or create case studies on your own. A case is a story of organizational issues that actually have been faced by people, together with facts, opinions, and prejudices on which decisions must be made.

In addition to the narrative, cases may include charts, graphs, and pictures of relevance to the situation. Case studies vary in length from a few paragraphs to book chapter length. They come with and without appendices. Some include discussion questions at the end in order to focus the reader's attention on certain issues. Others do not include questions, and part of the reader's challenge is to define the real issues of the case. Cases may be found in casebooks, as sections of textbooks, adapted from newspaper and magazine articles, on the Internet, created as fiction, or based on one's own life experience. Anyone can author a case. However, if a case is taken from another source, that source must be cited.

With the case method, the process of arriving at an answer is more important than the answer itself. By working through cases, you will develop an understanding of the process of reaching decisions and can support and communicate these decisions to others. Instead of sitting back and reacting to the comments made by an instructor, you will make decisions, typically with incomplete information and in a limited time period—the usual situation faced by most managers. No ideal solutions exist for any of the cases that will be presented to you. Searching for the perfect answer will be futile. Instead, you should learn to think through the issues, problems, facts, and other information presented in the cases. Critical thinking is required to make better decisions; thorough thinking is needed so that the decisions reached can be intelligently communicated. As such, discussions about the cases should clearly illustrate the thinking processes used.

The case method challenges you to consciously (a) describe what you have absorbed from the case, (b) analyze the facts, (c) synthesize what has been learned, (d) evaluate the data for qualitative and quantitative implications, and (e) apply that material in creating recommendations. The preparation for presentation, discussion, and written analysis of the cases could follow a set pattern. It is suggested that you:

1. Read the case rather quickly to get a feel for what is involved.
2. Reread the case and sort out the assumptions, hunches, and facts. Since most cases are incomplete, you can make plausible assumptions about the situation. List those assumptions and be able to support their plausibility. The assumptions enable you to "fill in the blanks" in the case. In organizations, decisions are generally made with incomplete information and some uncertainty.
3. Identify the major problems and subproblems that must be considered in the case.
4. List the problems in the order of their importance or priority. That is, show which problems must be solved first.
5. Develop a list of alternative courses of action that minimize or eliminate the problems. If possible, have at least two fully developed alternatives that are feasible solutions.
6. In developing alternative courses of action, outline the constraints (for example, resources, historical precedent, competition, skill limitations, attitudes) that limit success.
7. Select the best course of action for the problems identified in Step 3. Show how the course of action would work, and be able to discuss why it would be the most successful alternative for solving the problems.

Cases can be fun to write and to read. In addition, they provide another means by which we can learn about organizations and management, simulating real-life experience in the process.

Sample Guidelines for Student-Generated Cases

Case study preparation:

Provide a general description of a problem or issue you would like to work on. This can be related to a work project or problem that you have been asked to address that involves e-training or the development of a virtual work team: It can also be related to the development of an online course or training session in any setting. Discuss the following in your presentation:

- What are the specific issues in this case? What would you like help with?
- How are some of the issues we have been reading about and discussing reflected here?
- What are some initial ideas you have about this case or situation?
- Cases should be one to two pages in length. Please give each other feedback and engage in some discussion about the case! Please remember our guideline of confidentiality as we post and discuss these cases!

Collaborative work on cases:

Together you will choose four cases that you would like to discuss and develop more thoroughly. Your task will be to provide feedback on the issues outlined and provide solutions to any problems or concerns based on our reading and discussion. Depending on the number of students enrolled in the course, collaborative small groups may work on a case together and present the agreed-upon solution to the larger group. The small groups will negotiate their presentation date to the large group. If numbers enrolled in the course are smaller, we will initiate a discussion with you to decide how you would like to work on and present cases. All decisions about collaborative casework and presentations will be made during Week 6 of the course.

Evaluating Student Work

Evaluating students in an online course can be challenging, and explaining to students how they will be evaluated can be even more challenging. The following are two ways students can be appraised of how evaluation will happen. The first method is descriptive and can be incorporated into a course overview or syllabus.

It presents assignments and expectations that relate to grading at various levels. The second method is a grading rubric, which involves calculating points for discussion postings and papers (Exhibit A.1). The examples presented are for graduate-level courses. Should either form of grading be used with undergraduates, rationales for D grades would need to be developed and presented.

How You Will Be Evaluated?

Letter grades are given for this class: 70 percent of the grade is based on the formal assignments, and 30 percent based on other levels of interaction. Work quality is assessed on the basis of:

- Mastery of the readings
- Thoughtful and constructive responses and comments (the major source of feedback to your peers)
- Ability to remain calm, constructive, and resourceful in the face of conflict and turbulence

We have found that there are generally three levels of papers submitted in response to assignments. They are:

- Descriptive papers that simply describe or summarize material read.
- Analysis papers that compare and contrast theories or ideas. An analysis will break a theory into its component parts, describe the basic elements, and illustrate why those points are important. A good analysis will reorganize the material to create a summary that reflects on the important elements of the material and how they fit together.
- Synthesis papers that bring elements together and illustrate that the writer is engaging with the material being written about. A student writing a synthesis may agree or disagree with the material being read. The student may point out gaps in the material and will go far beyond a description of what this material means. A good synthesis demonstrates good critical thinking skills, engages the reader, and makes the reader think.

You will also called upon to write papers in response to the ideas and assignments of your student colleagues. These papers generally supplement what has been said, apply the material, critique the material being presented, or support what has been presented.

If we review both categories of papers by type and relate those to grades that would be applied in evaluation of the assignments, we come up with the following:

Assignments:

Describing or summarizing: B-
Analyzing: B+/A-
Synthesizing: A

Response papers and posting to discussion:

Supporting: B-
Applying or Supplementing: B/B+
Challenging or critiquing: B+/A-
Developing original thought: A

Papers in either category demonstrate the development of original thought. They are well written and grammatically correct.

In giving final grades for a course, we use the following rules of thumb:

Grade of A (-): This person made me think; shows insight and constructiveness of criticism, and flexibility.

Grade of B (+/-): This person handles the assignments adequately and posts assignments on time, with only a couple of exceptions.

Grade of C (+/-): This person misses some major points, shows some insensitivity, and has a pattern of late postings, but hangs in, persists, and doesn't let down the other student colleagues.

Grade of F: There are consistent problems, including late or nonexistent postings, poor feedback to colleagues, a tendency to focus on problems rather than solutions, and limited support to the group.

Please note: You will not be able to receive credit or the benefit of this course without participating in the online discussion. We will expect each of you to read and respond to the online discussion at least twice weekly. Consequently, if you are having technical or other difficulties with your participation, please contact one of us immediately.

EXHIBIT A.1.   SAMPLE GRADING RUBRIC.

Total Points and Course Grade

A total of 200 points may be earned in this course. A maximum of 100 points may be earned through Course Room participation and a maximum of 100 points may be earned in the final project.

180 to 200 points: A or S
160 to 179 points: B or S
159 points or less: C or I

Course Room Participation

Course Room participation points are divided into two categories: (1) responses to the discussion questions presented in each unit (50 points), and (2) responses to other learners (50 points).

Response to the Course Room discussion question (50 points):

45 to 50 points   1. A minimum length of 100–250 words per response.
2. Discussion is substantive and relates to key principles.
3. Uses personal/professional examples demonstrating application of principles.
4. Is submitted according to the deadlines in the course schedule.
5. Language is clear, concise, and easy to understand. Uses terminology appropriately and is logically organized

40 to 44 points   1. A length of 50–100 words per response.
2. Makes reference to key principles, but is not well developed or integrated in the response.
3. Refers to personal/professional examples, but is not well integrated in the response.
4. Submitted according to the deadlines in the course schedule.
5. Is adequately written, but may use some terms incorrectly; may need to be read two or more times to be understood.

35 to 39 points   1. Is less than 50 words.
2. Contains no reference to key principles; if key principles are present, there is no evidence the learner understood principles, or key principles are not integrated into the response.
3. There is no reference to personal/professional examples.
4. Response is not submitted by due date.
5. Poorly written; terms are used incorrectly; cannot comprehend learner's ideas after repeated readings.

Responses to other learners (50 points):

45 to 50 points   1. Is substantively related to and reinforces the unit overview, text, and/or supplementary readings.
2. Responds to the ideas and concerns of other learners.
3. Is characterized by three to four of the following criteria:
   a. thought-provoking
   b. supportive

      c. challenging

      d. reflective

  4. Is submitted according to deadlines in the course schedule.

  5. Language is clear, concise and easy to understand; uses terminology appropriately and is well organized.

40 to 44 points

1. Contains references to unit overview, text, and/or supplementary readings, but references are not well integrated in the response.
2. Response is peripherally related to the ideas and concerns of other learners.
3. Is characterized by one or two of the following criteria:
    a. thought-provoking
    b. supportive
    c. challenging
    d. reflective
4. Submitted according to deadlines in the course schedule
5. Adequately written, but may use some terms incorrectly; may need to be read two or more times to be understood.

35 to 39 points

1. Contains no reference to key principles; if key principles are present, there is no evidence learner understood principles, or key principles are not integrated in the response.
2. Response is unrelated to the ideas and concerns of other learners.
3. Response is not thought-provoking, supportive, challenging, or reflective.
4. Response is not submitted by due date.
5. Is poorly written; terms are used incorrectly; instructor cannot comprehend learner's ideas after repeated readings

Final Project

The final project is worth 100 points.

Position/hypothesis statement:

9 to 10 points	7 to 8 points	0 to 6 points
Includes a detailed description of the importance of the problem to be addressed. Includes a strong transition into the body of the literature review.	Statement is adequately developed; there is minimal transition to body of literature search.	Hypothesis is absent or poorly written. Does not provide a transition into body of literature review. Does not adequately describe the problem to be investigated.

Literature review, analysis, and critique:

27 to 30 points	24 to 26 points	0 to 23 points
Presents an insightful description of the literature. Clearly articulates the major	Provides adequate description of the literature. Presents some of the theoretical	Too few studies and theories are reviewed; some topic areas are omitted.

theoretical approaches. approaches and reviews
Provides insightful analysis a portion of the relevant
of the literature; assesses studies.
adequacy of published
studies. Studies reviewed
are relevant to the stated
problem or hypothesis.

Support of position or hypothesis:

27 to 30 points	24 to 26 points	0 to 23 points
Uses literature review and theories to support the position. Arguments presented are creative and present a number of original insights.	Adequately uses the literature review and theories; there is little evidence of a creative approach to the problem.	Ignores some significant and important theories and/or research. The literature is not used to support position or hypothesis.

Relation to professional practice:

18 to 20 points	16 to 17 points	0 to 15 points
Clear description of the reason for the problem and how it may benefit practitioners, the organization, and the community.	A small number of benefits are presented; it may be difficult to discern precisely why the problem is important.	Description of relationship is absent or not realistic.

Written communication:

9 to 10 points	7 to 8 points	0 to 6 points
Language is clear, concise, and easy to understand. Uses terminology appropriately and is well organized.	Is adequately written but may use some terms incorrectly; may need to be read two or more times to be understood.	Is poorly written; terms are used incorrectly; instructor cannot comprehend learner's ideas after repeated readings.

STUDENT TOOLS

Self-Assessment: Is Online Learning for Me?

The first section of this resource contains a sample self-assessment and a checklist for a student contemplating online learning. They are a compilation of several of the assessments found on various sites on the Internet. We offer them with a caution: if students score low on the assessment it is not necessarily a solid indicator that they will not do well in an online course. This assessment should be used as a guide only.

Self-Assessment Questions

How well would distance learning courses fit your circumstances and lifestyle? Circle an answer for each question and score as directed. Answer honestly—no one will see this but you!

1. My need to take this course now is:
    a. High—I need it immediately for a specific goal.
    b. Moderate—I could take it on campus later or substitute another course.
    c. Low—it could be postponed.

2. Feeling that I am part of a class is:

  a. Not particularly necessary to me.

  b. Somewhat important to me.

  c. Very important to me.

3. I would classify myself as someone who:

  a. Often get things done ahead of time.

  b. Needs reminding to get things done on time.

  c. Puts things off until the last minute or doesn't complete them.

4. Classroom discussion is:

  a. Rarely helpful to me.

  b. Sometimes helpful to me.

  c. Almost always helpful to me.

5. When an instructor hands out directions for an assignment, I prefer:

  a. Figuring out the instructions myself.

  b. Trying to follow the directions on my own, then asking for help as needed.

  c. Having the instructions explained to me.

6. I need faculty comments on my assignments:

  a. Within a few weeks, so I can review what I did.

  b. Within a few days, or I forget what I did.

  c. Right away, or I get very frustrated.

7. Considering my professional and personal schedule, the amount of time I have to work on a distance learning course is:

  a. More than enough for an on-campus course.

  b. The same as for a class on campus.

  c. Less than for a class on campus.

8. Coming to campus on a regular schedule is:

  a. Extremely difficult for me—I have commitments (work, family, or personal) during times when classes are offered.

  b. A little difficult, but I can rearrange my priorities to allow for regular attendance on campus.

  c. Easy for me.

9. As a reader, I would classify myself as:

  a. Good—I usually understand the text without help.

  b. Average—I sometimes need help to understand the text.

  c. Slower than average.

10. When I need help understanding the subject:

  a. I am comfortable approaching an instructor to ask for clarification.

  b. I am uncomfortable approaching an instructor, but do it anyway.

  c. I never approach an instructor to admit I don't understand something.

11. My ability to work with technology is as follows:

  a. I have excellent computer skills.

  b. I have some computer and Internet skills.

  c. I am not very familiar with a computer and do not feel comfortable surfing the Net.

Explanations

1. Distance learning students sometimes neglect their courses because of personal or professional circumstances. Having a compelling reason for taking the course helps motivate the student to stick with the course.

2. Some students prefer the independence of distance learning; others find the independence uncomfortable and miss being part of the classroom experience.

3. Distance learning courses give students greater freedom of scheduling, but they can require more self-discipline than on-campus classes.

4. Some people learn best by interacting with other students and instructors. Others learn better by listening, reading, and reviewing on their own. Some distance learning courses provide less opportunity for group interaction than most on-campus courses.

5. Distance learning requires you to work from written directions.

6. It may take as little as a couple of days or as much as two to three weeks to get comments back from your instructor in distance learning classes.

7. Distance learning requires at least as much time as on-campus courses or more. Students surveyed say that distance learning courses are as hard as or harder than on-campus courses.

8. Most people who are successful with distance learning find it difficult to come to campus on a regular basis because of their work/family/personal schedules.

9. Print materials are the primary source of directions and information in distance learning courses.

10. Students who do well in distance learning courses are usually comfortable contacting the instructor as soon as they need help with the course.

11. Students who do well in distance learning courses usually have some familiarity with the use of a computer and know how to access e-mail and the Internet.

Self-Assessment Checklist

1. I have access to a computer or the equipment required for an online class.
2. I am not intimidated by using technology for learning.
3. I feel comfortable using the computer for basic word processing, e-mail, and to access the Internet.
4. I am a good time manager, can meet deadlines, and can keep track of assignments.
5. I am an independent learner.
6. I am self-disciplined.
7. I can express my ideas, comments, questions, and emotions in writing.
8. I am generally flexible and can adjust to changing schedules.
9. I have some time available to go to campus, if required, for exams and meetings.
10. I am a self-starter.
11. I easily understand what I read.
12. I am goal-directed and often achieve my goals.
13. I am realistic and confident about my academic ability.
14. I am persistent and obstacles don't stop me.
15. I believe in taking responsibility for my own learning.
16. I am open to trying something new.
17. I am open to working in an unstructured setting.
18. I enjoy working in teams, doing collaborative projects, etc.

The more "yes" answers a student has to these questions, the higher likelihood of success in an online course.

Tips for Being a Successful Online Learner

Learning in the online environment is clearly different from taking classes in the face-to-face classroom. The following summarizes some tips to help you be as successful as possible in your courses and program:

- Log on to your courses at least twice weekly if not more. Assume that the first time you log on in a given week, it will be to make initial comments and see what others may have posted. Additional log-on time allows you to reflect and respond.

- Make sure that you are up to date on postings.
- Take responsibility for your own learning and plan to be a self-directed learner. Don't expect the instructor to provide you with all the information and direction you need in a course.
- Stay on top of your reading assignments and become good at research and analysis. Assume that taking initiative on your part will be positively received and will maximize your learning.
- Rely on and be responsible to your colleagues in a course. Be willing to provide good, constructive feedback to one another.
- If you feel lost or confused, ASK!!
- If you become upset or angry with something someone has posted, take a deep breath (or three or four!), wait twenty-four hours, and then respond. That posting generally looks very different the next day.
- Be prepared for the amount of time that online learning takes and make time for it in your week.
- Make sure to ask your family and friends for their support. You will need time to complete your work in this course—time that you may have to take away from them. Share your time management plan with them so that they understand the demands on your life now.
- Work on being flexible and patient. Life has a way of intruding in the online classroom that can sometimes be uncomfortable and trying. Technical issues and difficulties are also a part of that life. So "go with the flow" becomes an important mantra in this process! Remember that you are on the cutting edge of a new way of learning and earning a degree. Forging a new path can sometimes be difficult, but it can be less so if you flow with the challenges.
- Online learning is dynamic and exciting. You will learn not only about the material you are studying but also about the use of technology and how the use of technology can change the way you learn and interact. You will be developing new relationships in a new way. Enjoy it all!

Communication Tools

Here are a few of the most important online communication tools.

Emoticons

Emoticons (emotional icons) are used to compensate for the inability to convey voice inflections, facial expressions, and bodily gestures in written communication. Some emoticons are better known as "smileys." Emoticons can be very effective toward avoiding misinterpretation of the writer's intents. Although there are no standard definitions for the following emoticons, we have supplied their most usual meanings. Most emoticons will look like a face (eyes, nose, and mouth) when rotated ninety degrees clockwise.

:) or :-) Expresses happiness, sarcasm, or joke

:(or :-(Expresses unhappiness

:] or :-] Expresses jovial happiness

:[or :-[Expresses despondent unhappiness

:D or :-D Expresses jovial happiness

:I or :-I Expresses indifference

:-/ or :- Indicates undecided, confused, or skeptical. Also :/ or :<.

:Q or :-Q Expresses confusion

:S or :-S Expresses incoherence or loss of words

:</@> or :-</@> Expresses shock or screaming

:O or:-O Indicates surprise, yelling, or realization of an error ("uh oh!")

Acronyms

Acronyms are commonly used across the Internet to abbreviate communication. We do not encourage students to use acronyms in their discussion postings. However, when they are used, it is important to understand their meaning. We post these to assist everyone in understanding what is being said in online communication.

AAMOF As a matter of fact

BBFN Bye bye for now

BFN Bye for now

BTW By the way

BYKT But you knew that

CMIIW Correct me if I'm wrong

EOL End of lecture

FAQ Frequently asked question(s)

FITB Fill in the blank

FWIW For what it's worth

FYI For your information

HTH Hope this helps

IAC In any case

IAE In any event

IMCO In my considered opinion

IMHO In my humble opinion

IMNSHO In my not so humble opinion

IMO In my opinion

IOW In other words

LOL Lots of luck or laughing out loud

MHOTY My hat's off to you

NRN No reply necessary

OIC Oh, I see

OTOH On the other hand

ROF Rolling on the floor

ROFL Rolling on the floor laughing

ROTFL Rolling on the floor laughing

RSN Real soon now

SITD Still in the dark

TIA Thanks in advance

TIC Tongue in cheek

TTYL Talk to you later

TYVM Thank you very much

WYSIWYG What you see is what you get

<G> Grinning

<J> Joking

<L> Laughing

<S> Smiling

<Y> Yawning

Netiquette

Netiquette guidelines are an important component of the syllabus for an online course. To ensure that communication is professional and respectful, students need to be oriented to appropriate online communication. The following netiquette guidelines are adapted from those provided by Arlene Rinaldi, which can be found at [*http://www.fau.edu/netiquette/net/*]

Other sites where netiquette guidelines can be found are [*http://www.albion.com/netiquette/corerules.html*] and [*http://www.dtcc.edu/cs/rfc1855.html#1*].

Netiquette provides basic information about writing online, so you can do the following:

- Be properly understood.
- Get your points across effectively.
- Avoid getting anybody annoyed.
- Avoid looking like a "beginner" on the Net.

> One of the first rules you learn when you get online is: Don't write EVERY-THING IN UPPERCASE!
>
> Mixed-case text is more relaxing to read. See for yourself! HERE IS AN EXAMPLE OF A SENTENCE WRITTEN ENTIRELY IN UPPER-CASE! It may be easier to type that way, but it instantly tells everybody that you are new to the Net. Uppercase is sometimes used, when somebody wants to indicate that they are SHOUTING! But few people will read a message that SCREAMS at them.
>
> When typing in a message, break it up into paragraphs. People often skip enormous blocks of text. You do want them to read what you say, don't you?
>
> You should also put a blank line between paragraphs. This makes it easier to read.
>
> Keep it short. There is a lot of information on the net, and when people read what you've written, they want you to get to the point. They're busy, and they simply don't have the time to read a message in which you are "thinking out loud."
>
> Don't just make it up as you go along. Plan ahead.

So before you start to type, think first about what you want to say. Get your ideas straight in your head, and figure out how they all fit together. Then write it in as few words as possible.

Some people actually jot down notes before they type a message online. This helps them figure out what they need to say. Such people usually sound like they know what they're talking about, because their brief statements are never vague.

It's a good idea to use short paragraphs. This forces you to express yourself with a minimum of words. Also, bear in mind that it is harder to read text on a computer screen than in a book. Small paragraphs give the reader's eyes some relief.

Clarity

When you write something, make sure that people will understand you.

After you type in a message—and before you send it—try reading it out loud. Sometimes sentences that seem to be okay when you're typing don't really work when you read them back.

Avoid using acronyms. While some of these (such as BTW, which means "by the way") are well known, you can't be sure that all of your readers know what they mean. Net acronyms (BTW, ROFL, IIRC, IMNSHO, IANAL, etc.) may seem "hip" but if they confuse the reader, you may not get your point across.

Above all, avoid time-saving contractions, such as "ur" for "your," or "cya" for "see you later." When you use these, you're telling everybody that you can't type well enough to use complete words. Take a typing course if you have to—it will pay off very well in the years to come!

Note: Contractions may be appropriate in chat rooms, where fast typing is important. Still, do they save you that much time?

Quoting

This is the longest section in the guide, but it is one of the most important.

Many e-mail and message-board programs let you grab the entire message that another person has written and embed it in your reply. This is known as quoting. This feature, while useful, can actually make it less likely that people will read what you write.

Avoid Me-Tooing. Some people quote a huge message, then place a brief comment at the end, such as "I agree with this!" or "Me, too!" This can be annoying to the person who has to scroll all the way through the message, looking for the part that you wrote. It makes more sense for you to quote only a few important sentences that summarize the message adequately, and place your comment after that.

Actually, simply saying that you agree with something doesn't add much to the conversation. Why not tell people *why* you agree? You can state some of the reasons why you feel the way you do. This way, you will look like a thoughtful person who thinks carefully about things and considers all the facts.

Avoid Stepladdering. Sometimes people quote entire messages that contain quotes from earlier messages, which in turn contain quotes from still earlier messages. Message that contain "quotes in quotes in quotes" are said to be stepladdering.

Stepladdering is a serious problem, because by the time the reader gets to your text, it is not clear what you are commenting on.

Once again, you should extract only a few sentences that accurately represent the topic you are writing about. This saves the reader time, and ensures that the context of your reply is obvious.

Alternate Between Quotes and Your Comments. Sometimes it is not possible to find a few sentences in the original message that clearly convey what the writer was talking about. After all, the message may have covered several different topics. To make your replies more meaningful, alternate between carefully selected quotes and your comments.

Here is an example of selective quoting. The lines that start with the > symbol indicate text taken from the original message:

> So I said to him that Mac is better than Windows.
There is a comparison report in this month's issue of *Computer World*. It shows that each platform has unique advantages.

> The Mac interface was invented by Apple Computer.
Did you know that the Mac interface was based on a design from the Xerox PARC center?

> Still, Macs are better than PCs any day.
That really depends on what your application is, don't you think?

In this example, each comment is directly targeted at a specific comment made by the other person. Don't force your readers to guess at what part of the original message you are talking about.

There is no question that quoting effectively requires more effort than simply grabbing the entire text of what was written before. However, careful quoting will make your replies more organized, and your thoughts will come across more clearly.

When you use your valuable time to reply to a message, you want people to read and understand what you say. Don't let bad quoting habits make your messages unclear.

Why Bother? No matter how clever or intelligent you are, if you spell badly, people will take your words less seriously. That may not be fair, but that's the way it is on the net.

Most computers have one or more spell-check programs. Some of them even have spell-checkers built right in to the e-mail or browser software you are using. You owe it to yourself to learn how these work.

When you go to a party or reception, you take the time to make sure that you look your best. Well, people on the Net don't know how beautiful you are—they can only see what you type. So take the time to make sure that what you write makes you look good.

By the way, spell-check programs are not perfect. They tend to miss mistakes like this: "Always right your sentences carefully." So even if you spell-check your text, it's a good idea to read it over before you send it.

Note: The Net is available almost everywhere in the world. Sometimes people may appear ignorant or uneducated because of bad spelling. Bear in mind, though, that they may not be writing in their native language.

Manners. There are many ways to get people on the Net annoyed with you, even if you are usually a polite person.

The worst problem is something called "keyboard bravery." When you are sitting comfortably in front of your computer, safe from the world, it is often tempting to write a message that is so harshly phrased that it is insulting. Everybody has, at times, felt like writing a scathing message.

The usual explanation for this behavior is "I'm just telling people what I think!" or "I'm only being honest!" Well, that may be true, but if you are not careful, you can offend somebody, and that can start an argument that benefits no one.

If you frequently get into nasty debates, you should visit a search engine and look for the word "netiquette." Much has been written about the importance of behaving diplomatically while online.

You should always read what you have written before you send your message. This will not only help you spot errors in spelling, phrasing, and grammar, but also may help you notice that you don't sound as friendly as you would like.

Feedback Guidelines

Note: The following feedback guidelines are an abbreviated version of netiquette guidelines that assist students in understanding what is meant by giving and receiving good feedback. Students rarely intuitively know how to give good feedback. Consequently, teaching them how to do so assists them in meeting course objectives and has the secondary advantage of promoting the development of critical thinking skills.

- Don't just make feedback up as you go along. Plan ahead.
- Before you start to type, think first about what you want to say. Get your ideas straight in your head, and figure out how they all fit together.
- Make some notes before typing a message online. This helps you figure out what you need to say.

- Use short paragraphs. This forces you to express yourself with a minimum of words.
- When you write something, make sure that people will understand you. After you type in a message—and before you send it—try reading it out loud. Sometimes sentences that seem to be OK when you're typing don't really work when you read them back
- Some people quote a huge message, then place a brief comment at the end, such as "I agree with this!" or "Me, too!" This can be annoying to the person who has to scroll all the way through the message, looking for the part that you wrote. It makes more sense for you to quote only a few important sentences that summarize the message adequately, and place your comment after that.
- Simply saying that you agree with something doesn't add much to the conversation. Again, why not tell people why you agree and then state some of the reasons that you feel the way you do?
- Always read what you have written before you send your message. Not only will this help you spot errors in spelling, phrasing, and grammar, but you may also notice that you don't sound as friendly as you would like. Make sure your message is worded professionally and not harshly to avoid insulting those who will read it and inadvertently "flaming" other members of the group.

Time Management Tips and Tools

The ability to manage your time is a critical factor in your ability to be successful in an online course. The following tools will allow you to establish your goals and then set priorities and schedules for managing your time. The tools are not mandatory for you to use, but they may be useful if you find you are getting behind or feeling overwhelmed.

Some general tips for managing your time in an online course:

- Log on to the course site daily or every other day with the intention of reading only.
- Prepare your first post for the week in response to the discussion questions posed by the instructor or student facilitator—these should be your original ideas. So wait until *after* you have posted your response to begin reading the responses of your student colleagues.
- Print new messages if you need to in order to give yourself time to review them at your leisure.
- Once you have read and reviewed what's new, formulate your response *off-line* using your word processing program. This gives you time to think about what you want to say as well as to check your grammar and spelling. Do not feel that an immediate response is necessary—you can take your time!

- Once you have composed your response, copy and paste it to the course site.

The following are a couple of tools that may help you set goals and manage your time in an online course.

Goal Inventory

When thinking about your goals for learning, it is also important to consider how learning fits into the rest of your life. Begin by thinking about what you'd like to achieve over the next few years in each area of your life, potential obstacles that may inhibit your progress, and the initial steps you think you can take to get to where you want to be (Exhibit B.1).

Now that you have established your longer-term goals, what do you hope to accomplish during the next school term in each area? Prioritize them from most important to least important.

Your priorities are set! How will you structure your time so that you meet your short-term goals and priorities? Following are a weekly objectives list, a weekly planner, and a time summary sheet that you may choose to use in managing your time. Some people find these tools constraining. If so, find another way to structure and monitor your time that feels comfortable for you. Also, remember that life will intervene in the best of plans. So don't get so locked into a schedule that you are unable to accommodate the interferences that are likely to occur. *Remember: flexibility is the key to success in online learning!*

Once you have your objectives for the week established (Exhibit B.2), along with the time necessary to complete them, calendar the time on a weekly planner (Exhibit B.3).

EXHIBIT B.1. LIFE GOALS.

Life or Area	Goals	Potential Obstacles	Initial Steps to Achieve Goals
School			
Work			
Family			
Friends			
Personal			
Other			

EXHIBIT B.2.   WEEKLY OBJECTIVES.

Weekly Objectives			
Objective	Activity to Complete	Time Estimated to Complete	Completed? Yes? No? Partially?

So how did you do? Review your use of time for the week by using the Weekly Summary of Time Use (Exhibit B.4).

Although this may seem like a cumbersome process, once you get into the habit of budgeting your time weekly, the amount of time you will need for planning will decrease and time management will become a habit.

EXHIBIT B.3.   WEEKLY PLANNER.

Weekly Planner							
	Monday	Tuesday	Wednesday	Thursday	Friday	Saturday	Sunday
8–9							
9–10							
10–11							
11–12							
12–1							
1–2							
2–3							
3–4							
4–5							
5–6							
6–7							
7–8							

EXHIBIT B.4. WEEKLY SUMMARY OF TIME USE.

Weekly Summary of Time Use								
	Sleep	Eat	Commute	Family/ Friends	Study	Work	Play	Other
Monday								
Tuesday								
Wednesday								
Thursday								
Friday								
Saturday								
Sunday								

Writing Research and Reflection Papers

We have found that students often need much guidance in the preparation and presentation of research and reflection papers. The following questions to consider in writing a research paper are an adaptation of work provided by Jeremy Shapiro at the Fielding Graduate Institute. This is followed by tips we have created for writing a research paper. In addition, we offer guidelines for the creation of a reflection paper that may be submitted either midterm or at the end of an online course as a self-evaluation piece.

Research Papers

Questions to consider in writing a research paper:

1. Why am I including this material?
2. What is the context for this work?
3. Have I constructed good transitions between ideas and sections?
4. Do my ideas follow a logical flow? Is the paper well organized?
5. Have I presented good evidence for my thoughts? Stated the strengths and weaknesses of my argument and the arguments in the literature?
6. What evidence do I have for my ideas?

7. Have I used references and formatted them appropriately using APA or another style guide?
8. Have I used good grammar and complete sentences, and checked my spelling?
9. Have I defined all words or phrases?
10. Have I cited appropriately, giving credit for direct quotations and paraphrases?

Some other tips for research papers:

- Use *subheads* to set apart sections of text: they make you think twice about what you want to say and provide a list of the main points you want to get across, and they provide a guide or road signs for the reader.
- Remember to use subheads that are consistent with the content contained beneath them. One mistake often made is to compose creative subheads that do not relate to the content at all. That is not helpful for the reader.
- Provide an *abstract* at the beginning of the paper. It creates context and lets the reader know "Why am I reading this?" In general, when writing a paper, it is fine to use your own voice and avoid academic jargon. Don't be afraid to use "I" or "This author" when expressing your own opinion about a topic. But be sure to use parallel syntax for each point made. In other words, if using "I," don't revert to the third person in the next point or idea. Be consistent!
- Create a solid *introduction* section that sets the stage for the body of the paper. Your introduction should let the reader know the basis and rationale for your work and should provide important background information on the topic.
- When appropriate, include a *methods* section that informs the reader of the ways in which you conducted your research. Was it a literature review or did you do some interviews or use other means by which you gathered information for your paper?
- The *discussion* sections of your paper should elaborate on the various aspects of the topic and should demonstrate your command and understanding of the material. This is where subheads are particularly helpful in delineating the various topics that form the whole of your paper.
- Provide a good, solid *conclusions* section that ties all of your ideas together and perhaps points to ideas for further study. This is probably the most difficult part of the paper to write, so once you have covered all of your ideas, let the paper sit for a day or so to allow you to reflect on your conclusions.

Writing Reflection Papers

There are two types of reflection papers that you may be asked to write for a course. The first relates to the material studied in the course and should contain three elements:

- A summary of ideas
- An analysis of concepts
- A synthesis of thoughts and evidence of original thought

Here are some questions to consider when completing the three sections of a reflection paper related to course material:

Summary of Ideas

- What is the context for the information read or discussed?
- What information was presented in the reading or in course discussion?
- What are the key points of the arguments both pro and con?

Analysis of Concepts

- What are the strengths and weaknesses of the ideas presented?
- Are there gaps or omissions?
- What are the implications of this work?
- What are the chief influences on this work and how are they manifested within it?
- How did the context of this work influence the outcome?

Synthesis of Ideas

- In summarizing and analyzing this work, what new ideas have emerged for me?
- What is my opinion or how do I view this material?
- What are some new areas of study that are indicated by this work?
- What criticisms do I have of this work?
- What do I see as the strengths or contributions of this work to the field as a whole?
- If gaps or omissions exist, how might they be filled?

Tips for Writing Self-Reflections

You may also be asked to write a final reflection of your overall learning process in the course. This is your opportunity to reflect on your learning, to evaluate the process, and to provide suggestions to the instructor for course improvement. When writing a reflection paper as an evaluation of your learning and the course, consider the following:

- Who was I as a learner before I entered this course?
- Have I changed? If so, how?

- How has my participation in this course changed my learning process or my view of myself as a learner?
- What have I gained (or not) by participating in this course?
- Have I learned anything new about the topic or myself?
- What suggestions do I have for future groups participating in this course or for the instructor of this course?
- Would I recommend this course to my friends and colleagues? Why or why not?
- How do I evaluate my own contributions to the course? What grade would I give myself?

REFERENCES

Alley, J., and Jansak, K. "The Ten Keys to Quality Assurance and Assessment in Online Learning." *Journal of Instruction Development*, Winter 2001, *1*(3), pp. 3–18.

American Association of University Professors. "Distance Education and Intellectual Property." *Academe*, May-June 1999, pp. 41–45.

American Association of University Women. *The Third Shift: Women Learning Online*. Washington, D.C.: American Association of University Women, 2001.

American Council on Education. "Developing a Distance Education Policy for 21st-Century Learning." Mar. 2000. [http://www.acenet.edu/washington/distance_ed/2000/03march/distance_ed.htm].

Armstrong, T. *Multiple Intelligences in the Classroom*. Alexandria, Va.: Association for Supervision and Curriculum Development, 1994.

Angelo, T., and Cross, K. P. *Classroom Assessment Techniques*. San Francisco: Jossey-Bass, 1993.

Bates, A. W. *Managing Technological Change*. San Francisco: Jossey-Bass, 2000.

Belenky, M. F., Clinchy, B. M., Goldberger, N. R., and Tarule, J. M. *Women's Ways of Knowing: The Development of Self, Voice, and Mind*. New York: Basic Books, 1986.

Boud, D., and Griffin, V. *Appreciating Adults Learning: From the Learner's Perspective*. London, England: Kogan Page, 1987.

Brookfield, S. D. *Developing Critical Thinkers: Challenging Adults to Explore Alternative Ways of Thinking and Acting*. San Francisco: Jossey-Bass, 1987.

Brookfield, S. D. *Becoming a Critically Reflective Teacher*. San Francisco: Jossey-Bass, 1995.

Brookfield, S. D., and Preskill, S. *Discussion as a Way of Teaching*. San Francisco: Jossey-Bass, 1999.

Brown, R. "The Process of Community-Building in Distance Learning Classes." *JALN*, *5*(2), Sept. 2001. [http://www.aln.org/alnweb/journal/Vol5_issue2/Brown/Brown.htm].

Buchanan, E. "Going the Extra Mile: Serving Distance Education Students with Resources and Services." *Syllabus*, May 2000, pp. 44–47.

Byers, C. "Interactive Assessment and Course Transformation Using Web-Based Tools." *The Technology Source*, May-June 2002. [http://ts.mivu.org/default.asp?show=article&id=928].

Callan, J. M. "Attitudes Toward Computers: The Changing Gender Gap." *Feminist Collections: A Quarterly of Women's Studies Resources*, Jan. 31, 1996, *17*(2), pp. 30–32.

Carnevale, D. "Should Distance Students Pay for Campus-Based Services?" *Chronicle of Higher Education*, Sept. 14, 2001. [http://chronicle.com/weekly/v48/i03/03a03501.htm].

Carr, S. "As Distance Learning Comes of Age, the Challenge Is Keeping the Students." *Chronicle of Higher Education*, Feb. 11, 2000. [http://www.chronicle.com/free/v46/i23/23a00101.htm].

Carr-Chellman, A., and Ducastel, P. "The Ideal Online Course." *Library Trends*, 2001, *50*(1), p. 16.

Chickering A., and Gamson, Z. "Seven Principles of Good Practice in Undergraduate Education." *AAHE Bulletin*, 1987, *39*, pp. 3–7.

Christiansen, E., and Dirckinck-Holmfeld, L. "Making Distance Learning Cooperative," 1995. [http://www.csc195.indiana.edu/csc195/chritia.html].

Claxton, C. S., and Murrell, P. H. *Learning Styles*. Washington, D.C.: ERIC Clearinghouse on Higher Education, 1988.

Collison, G., Elbaum, B., Haavind, S., and Tinker, R. *Facilitating Online Learning: Effective Strategies for Moderators*. Madison, Wis.: Atwood, 2000.

Daniel, J. "Lessons from the Open University: Low-Tech Learning Often Works Best." *Chronicle of Higher Education*, Sept. 7, 2001. [http://chronicle.com/weekly/v48/i02/02b02401.htm].

Diaz, D. "Online Drop Rates Revisited." *The Technology Source*, May/June 2002. [http://ts.mivu.org/default.asp?show=article&id=981].

Donald, J. G. *Learning to Think: Disciplinary Perspectives*. San Francisco: Jossey-Bass, 2002.

Everhart, R. "Creating Services for Connected Learners." *Syllabus*, May 2000, pp. 48–50.

Fidishun, D. "Andragogy and Technology: Integrating Adult Learning Theory as We Teach with Technology." Retrieved April 4, 2002. [http://www.mtsu.edu/~itconf/proceed00/fidishun.htm].

Gardner, H. *Frames of Mind*. New York: Basic Books, 1983.

Gilbert, S. D. *How to Be a Successful Online Student*. New York: McGraw-Hill, 2001.

Gillett, M. "Advancing on Technology: Are Women Gaining Ground?" *Women's Times*, Nov. 30, 1996, *4*(3), p. 1.

Goldsmith, D. J. "Communication, Humor, and Personality: Students' Attitudes to Learning Online." *Academic Exchange Quarterly*, 2001, *5*(2), p. 108.

Graham, C., Kursat, C., Byung-Ro, L., Craner, J., and Duffy, T. "Seven Principles of Effective Teaching: A Practical Lens for Evaluating Online Courses." *The Technology Source*, Mar.-Apr. 2001. Retrieved September 5, 2002. [http://ts.mivu.org/default.sap?show=article&id=839].

Hanna, D. E., Glowaki-Dudka, M., and Conceição-Runlee, S. *147 Practical Tips for Teaching Online Groups*. Madison, Wis.: Atwood, 2000.

Hara, N., and Kling, K. "Students' Distress with a Web-Based Distance Learning Course: An Ethnographic Study of Participants' Experiences." Spring 2000. Retrieved September 3, 2002. [http://www.slis.indiana.edu/CSI/Wp/wp00~01B.html].

Harasim, L., Hiltz, S. R., Teles, L., and Turoff, M. *Learning Networks*. Cambridge, Mass.: MIT Press, 1996.

Harris, R. "Preventing and Detecting Plagiarism." *The Plagiarism Handbook: Strategies for Preventing, Detecting, and Dealing with Plagiarism* (pp. 61–82). Los Angeles, Calif.: Pyrczak, 2002. [http://www.antiplagiarism.com/generic7.html].

Hase, S., and Kenyon, C. "From Andragogy to Heutagogy." *UltiBASE Articles,* Dec. 2000. Retrieved April 4, 2002. [http://ultibase.rmit.edu.au/Articles/dec00/hase2.htm].

Hawke, C. *Computer and Internet Use on Campus: A Legal Guide to Issues of Intellectual Property, Free Speech, and Privacy.* San Francisco: Jossey-Bass, 2001.

Henderson, L. "Instructional Design of Interactive Multimedia: A Cultural Critique." *Educational Technology Research and Development,* 1996, *44*(4), 85–104.

Herring, S. "Gender and Democracy in Computer-Mediated Communication." 1993. [http://www.cios.org/getfile/HERRING_V3N293].

Herring, S. "Gender Differences in Computer-Mediated Communication: Bringing Familiar Baggage to the New Frontier." 1994. [http://www.cpsr.org/gender/herring.txt].

Hudson, B. "Critical Dialogue Online: Personas, Covenants, and Candlepower." In K. E. Rudestam and J. Schoenholtz-Read (eds.), *Handbook of Online Learning* (pp. 53–90). Thousand Oaks, Calif.: Sage, 2002.

Illinois Online Network. "What Makes a Successful Online Student?" Retrieved April 7, 2002. [wysiwyg://90/http://www.ion.illinois.ed.rces/onlineLearning/StudentProfile.htm].

Irving, L. *Falling Through the Net: Toward Digital Inclusion.* Washington, D.C.: National Telecommunications and Information Administration, 1995. [http://www.ntia.doc.gov/ntiahome/fttn00/contents00.html].

Joo, J. "Cultural Issues of the Internet in Classrooms." *British Journal of Educational Technology,* July 1999, *30*(3), pp. 245–250.

Kellogg, A. P. "Students Plagiarize Less Than Many Think, a New Study Finds." *Chronicle of Higher Education,* Feb. 1, 2002. [http://chronicle.com/free/2002/02/2002020101t.htm].

King, L. "Gender Issues in Online Communities." *CSPR Newsletter,* Winter 2000, *18*(1).

Kirton, G., and Greene, A. "Women Learning Online: Overcoming the Gendered Temporal and Spatial Barriers to Women's Trade Union Participation?" Paper presented to Unions and the Internet conference, May 11, 2001. Retrieved June 2, 2002. [http://www.geocities.com/e_collectivism/e_learning.htm].

Knowles, M. *The Adult Learner: A Neglected Species.* Houston, Tex.: Gulf, 1992.

Litzinger, M., and Osif, B., "Accommodating Diverse Learning Styles: Designing Instruction for Electronic Information Sources." In L. Shirato (ed.), *What Is Good Instruction Now? Library Instruction for the '90s.* Ann Arbor, Mich.: Pierian Press, 1993.

Market Data Retrieval. *College Technology Review, 2001–2002.* Shelton, Conn.: Market Data Retrieval, Jan. 2002.

Mayes, C. "Learning Technology and Learning Relationships." In J. Stephenson (ed.), *Teaching and Learning Online: Pedagogies for New Technologies.* London, England: Kogan Page, 2001.

McClure, B. *Putting a New Spin on Groups.* Hillsdale, N.J.: Erlbaum, 1998.

McLoughlin, C. "Culturally Responsive Technology Use: Developing an On-Line Community of Learners." *British Journal of Educational Technology,* July 1999, *30*(3), pp. 231–243.

Mezirow, J. *Fostering Critical Reflection in Adulthood: A Guide to Transformative and Emancipatory Learning.* San Francisco: Jossey-Bass, 1990.

Morgan, C., and O'Reilly, M. *Assessing Open and Distance Learners.* London, England: Kogan Page, 1999.

Muilenburg, L., and Berge, Z. L., "A Framework for Designing Questions for Online Learning," DEOSNEWS, 2000, *10*(2). [http://www.emoderators.com/moderators/muilenburg.htm].

National Center for Education Statistics. *National Postsecondary Student Aid Study, 1999–2000.* Washington, D.C.: U.S. Department of Education, National Center for Education Statistics, June 6, 2002. [http://nces.ed.gov/surveys/npsas/table_library/tables/npsas23.asp]. [http://nces.ed.gov/surveys/npsas/table_library/tables/npsas22.asp].

O'Connor, T. *Using Learning Styles to Adapt Technology for Higher Education.* Indiana State University Center for Teaching and Learning, Feb. 21, 1997. [http://web.indstate.edu/ctl/styles/learning.html].

O'Reilly, M., and Newton, D. "Why Interact Online If It's Not Assessed?" *Academic Exchange Quarterly,* 2001, *5*(4), p. 70.

Palloff, R. *Confronting Ghosts: Lessons in Empowerment and Action.* Unpublished doctoral dissertation, Human and Organizational Systems, Fielding Graduate Institute, 1996.

Palloff, R., and Pratt, K. *Building Learning Communities in Cyberspace: Effective Strategies for the Online Classroom.* San Francisco: Jossey-Bass, 1999.

Palloff, R., and Pratt, K. *Lessons from the Cyberspace Classroom: The Realities of Online Teaching.* San Francisco: Jossey-Bass, 2001.

Palloff, R., and Pratt, K., "Beyond the Looking Glass: What Faculty and Students Need to Be Successful Online." In K. E. Rudestam and J. Schoenholtz-Read (eds.), *Handbook of Online Learning* (pp. 171–184). Thousand Oaks, Calif.: Sage, 2002.

Paulsen, M. F. "The Online Report on Pedagogical Techniques for Computer-Mediated Communication." DEOSNEWS, 1995. [http://www.nettskolen.com/forskning/19/cmcped.html].

Peterson, P. W. "The Debate About Online Learning: Key Issues for Writing Teachers." *Computers and Composition,* 2001, *18*(4), 359–370.

Phipps, R., and Merisotis, J. *What's the Difference?* Washington, D.C.: Institute for Higher Education Policy, Apr. 1999.

Pratt, K. *The Electronic Personality.* Unpublished doctoral dissertation, Human and Organizational Systems, Fielding Graduate Institute, 1996.

Preece, J. *Online Communities: Designing Usability, Supporting Sociability.* New York: Wiley, 2000.

Primo, L. H., and Lesage, T. "Survey of Intellectual Property Issues for Distance Learning and Online Educators." *USDLA ED Magazine,* Feb. 2001, *15*(2). [http://www.usdla.org/ED_magazine/illuminactive/FEB01_Issue/article03.html].

Rheingold, H. *The Virtual Community.* Reading, Mass.: Addison-Wesley, 1993.

Schroeder, C. "New Students—New Learning Styles." *Change,* Sept.-Oct. 1993. [http://www.virtualschool.edu/mon/Academia/KierseyLearningStyles.html].

Shapiro, A. L. *The Control Revolution.* New York: Century Foundation, 1997.

Shapiro, J. J., and Hughes, S. K. "The Case of the Inflammatory E-Mail: Building Culture and Community in Online Academic Environments." In K. E. Rudestam and J. Schoenholtz-Read (eds.), *Handbook of Online Learning* (pp. 91–124). Thousand Oaks, Calif.: Sage, 2002.

Standen, P. J., Brown, D. J., and Cromby, J. J. "The Effective Use of Virtual Environments in the Education and Rehabilitation of Students with Intellectual Disabilities." *British Journal of Educational Technology,* June 2001, *32*(3), pp. 289–299.

Strong, R. W., and Harmon, E. G. "Online Graduate Degrees: A Review of Three Internet-Based Master's Degree Offerings." *American Journal of Distance Education,* 1997, *11*(3), pp. 58–70.

Truong, H. "Gender Issues in Online Communications." 1993. [http://students.cec.wustl.edu/~cs142/articles/GENDER_ISSUES/gender_issues_in_online_communications—bawit].

Vu, C. "According to Women of Color, There's No Need to Fear Technology." *Northwest Asian Weekly,* June 2, 2000, *19*(22), p. 1.

Weimer, M. *Learner-Centered Teaching.* San Francisco: Jossey-Bass, 2002.

Wenger, E. *Communities of Practice: Learning, Meaning, and Identity.* Cambridge, England: Cambridge University Press, 1999.

Young, J. "Experts Say Technology Gap Among Colleges Perpetuates 'Digital Divide' in Society." *Chronicle of Higher Education,* June 21, 2002. [http://chronicle.com/weekly/ v48/4841guide.htm].

~

INDEX